Facing the Past

Nineteenth-Century Portraits from the Collection of the Pennsylvania Academy of the Fine Arts

•

Susan Danly

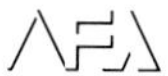

The American Federation of Arts

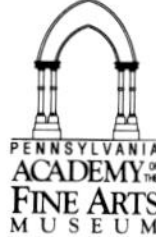

Pennsylvania Academy of the Fine Arts

This catalogue has been published in conjunction with *Facing the Past: Nineteenth-Century Portraits from the Collection of the Pennsylvania Academy of the Fine Arts*, an exhibition organized by the Pennsylvania Academy of the Fine Arts with the support of the National Endowment for the Arts, a federal agency. Research for this project was funded with support from The Henry Luce Foundation, Inc. Circulated by the American Federation of Arts, the exhibition is a project of ART ACCESS, a program of the AFA with major support from the Lila Wallace-Reader's Digest Fund.

Published by the American Federation of Arts,
41 East 65th Street, New York, New York 10021,
and the Pennsylvania Academy of the Fine Arts,
118 North Broad Street, Philadelphia, Pennsylvania 19102

Library of Congress Cataloging-in-Publication Data

Danly, Susan
Facing the past: nineteenth century portraits from the collection of the Pennsylvania Academy of the Fine Arts / Susan Danly.
p. cm.
Catalog of an exhibit circulated by the American Federation of Arts.
Includes bibliographical references and index.
ISBN 0-943836-16-6
1. Portrait painting, American—Exhibitions. 2. Portrait painting—19th century—United States—Exhibitions. 3. Portraits, American—Exhibitions. 4. Portrait miniatures, American—Exhibitions. 5. United States—Biography—Portraits—Exhibitions. 6. Pennsylvania Academy of the Fine Arts—Exhibitions.
I. Pennsylvania Academy of the Fine Arts. II. American Federation of Arts. III. Title.
ND1311.2.D36 1992
757'.0973'074—dc20—50 92-2721
CIP

Publication Coordinator: Michaelyn Mitchell
Design: Lawrence Wolfson
Editor: Jacolyn A. Mott
Photographer: Rick Echelmeyer
Composition: The Sarabande Press
Cover Design: Lawrence Wolfson
Printed in Hong Kong by South China Printing

Contents

Foreword

The Pennsylvania Academy of the Fine Arts has long been known for its rich holdings of early nineteenth-century portraits by members of the Peale family, Gilbert Stuart, Thomas Sully, John Neagle, and Jacob Eichholtz. During the past ten years, the scope of the portrait collection has been deliberately broadened to include a wider range of geographic regions and historical styles. In 1984, for example, the Academy purchased an important work by the leading painter in colonial New England, John Singleton Copley: the portrait *Robert "King" Hooper* was executed in 1767 in Boston. Copley was a major inspiration to Charles Willson Peale; and together they established portraiture as the preeminent art form of their time. Henry Benbridge's ambitious conversation piece *The Gordon Family*, of about 1762, was acquired in 1987. It shows the degree of sophistication that marked the rise of portrait painting in Philadelphia. These group portraits, which had their origins in seventeenth-century Dutch painting and flourished in eighteenth-century England, became very popular in Philadelphia with artists like Charles Willson Peale, James Peale, and Edward Savage. Two early nineteenth-century folk, or "plain style," portraits by unidentified artists, given to the Academy in 1980, have proved to have unexpected significance. Now attributed to Joshua Johnson, one of the earliest African-American artists, these paintings provide a valuable link between the academic tradition as practiced by the Peale family and the art of the self-taught limner.

Throughout the nineteenth century, many works were given by descendants of the sitters and by local collectors who recognized the Pennsylvania Academy's important role in the exhibiting of portraits and the teaching of portrait painting. This revival of interest in portraiture in the latter part of the nineteenth century is reflected in the collection by naturalist works by Thomas Eakins and his circle and works by William Merritt Chase, Robert Vonnoh, and Cecilia Beaux. Because these artists both taught and exhibited at the Pennsylvania Academy, they had a considerable impact on the local art community. Their works, along with those of other fashionable society portraitists like Thomas P. Anshutz and John McLure Hamilton were purchased by the Pennsylvania Academy from its prestigious annual exhibitions or given by donors who wanted to recognize these artists' special contribution to American art or the sitters' importance to history.

This exhibition and catalogue provide, for the first time, an overview of the Pennsylvania Academy's nineteenth-century portrait collection. Funded by generous grants from the National Endowment for the Arts, a federal agency, and the Henry Luce Foundation, *Facing the Past* is the third and final project in a series designed to feature important aspects of the Academy's history. In order to make this history known to a broad constituency of museum visitors, the exhibition will travel under the auspices of the American Federation of Arts, directed by Serena Rattazzi. We are particularly grateful to her and her staff who have overseen the production of the catalogue and the national tour.

The project has been realized with the participation of the entire staff of the Pennsylvania Academy. It was conceived by Susan Danly, curator of collections, who coordinated all the details. Jacolyn A. Mott, editor in chief, edited the catalogue for the Academy; and Tamsin Wolff, education specialist, helped create the related educational components.

Linda Bantel
The Edna S. Tuttleman Director of the Museum
Pennsylvania Academy of the Fine Arts

Acknowledgments

The staff of the AFA is delighted to present once again an exhibition drawn from the rich holdings of the Pennsylvania Academy of the Fine Arts. The last in a series of three collaborations between the two institutions, *Facing the Past* includes an outstanding group of works created in a variety of portrait types. Our thanks go to Linda Bantel, director of the Academy, for her continuing support, and to Susan Danly, curator, for the thoughtful perspective she provides in this catalogue and for the high degree of professionalism with which she carried out her many curatorial duties. At the AFA, much hard work was put into the project by Thomas Padon, Associate Curator of Exhibitions, and Michaelyn Mitchell, Head of Publications. Others whose important roles should be singled out include J. David Farmer, Director of Exhibitions; Robert Workman, Assistant Director of Exhibitions; Carol Farra, Registrar; Julie Min, Exhibition Scheduler; and Jillian W. Slonim, Public Information Director. Our deep appreciation goes to the Lila Wallace-Reader's Digest Fund for their support through the AFA's ART ACCESS program.

Serena Rattazzi, *Director, The American Federation of Arts*

The study of nineteenth-century American portraiture reveals a great deal about changes in artistic style during an especially dynamic period in our nation's history. Portraits also help us understand more about how specific individuals have come to represent types of class and gender. My appreciation of American portraiture has been greatly enhanced through contact with an important collection of British art, at the Huntington Library and Art Gallery in San Marino, California. Robert Wark, former curator of the collection, provided a model of scholarship in lectures and writings that opened many eyes to the complexity and vitality of portraiture as a genre. I am most grateful to the Huntington Library for a research grant which allowed me to examine the development of American painting within the context of that rich British tradition. In addition, general discussions on the social role of American portraiture with Lillian B. Miller of the National Portrait Gallery in Washington, D. C., Paul Staiti of Mount Holyoke College in Holyoke, Massachusetts, and Susan Rather of the University of Texas at Austin have helped to shape my thoughts on this subject.

Other individuals have generously shared their knowledge about specific American artists and their subjects: Tara Tappert on Cecilia Beaux; Paul W. Richelson, former curator at the Grand Rapids Art Museum, on William Merritt Chase; Mrs. Charles E. Dunbar and Renée V. Overholser, descendants of Victor Value, on the sitters in the Jacob Eichholtz painting; David Tatham of Syracuse University and Thomas Hunter, assistant director of the Onondaga Historical Association in Syracuse, New York, on Charles Loring Elliott; John Wilmerding of Princeton University and Joy Peto Smiley on the Peto family; Mark Thistlethwaite on Peter Rothermel; and E. Richard McKinstry of the Winterthur Library on the Thomas Sully manuscript in its collection.

No exhibition would ever come to fruition without the skill and effort of the museum's staff. I would especially like to thank Tamsin Wolff, the education specialist on this project, who consistently reminded me of the varied needs and interests of our audience. Mark Bockrath, Barbara Wojcek, and Robin Beckett in the conservation department worked diligently to present these portraits and their frames in the best light. The Pennsylvania Academy's able archivist, Cheryl Leibold, and a summer intern, Meghan Duffy, aided my research for this catalogue; Judy Hayman Moore coordinated the photography. Serena Orteca and Susan James-Gadzinski assisted with the production of labels and proofreading. And, finally, Tim Gilfillan and his crew put it all on the walls. A longtime supporter of the Pennsylvania Academy and its exhibition programs, James F. O'Gorman has once again provided his valued services as a careful reader and critic of this manuscript.

Susan Danly, *Curator*

The Portrait Tradition at the Pennsylvania Academy of the Fine Arts

It is good to go and see these portraits. Life consists of meeting and dealing with people. We are interested more in the personages of the past than in the dry details of history.

Philadelphia *Inquirer* (Nov. 22, 1905)

This review of an exhibition held at the Pennsylvania Academy of the Fine Arts almost a hundred years ago touches on the fundamental appeal of portraiture. Looking at portraits is a means of facing our past. While portraits provide both a lasting record of a person's physical features and often his or her personality, they can convey broader social and aesthetic meaning, as well. Portraits often draw attention to the social status, gender role, professional accomplishments, or personal interests of a sitter. Portraits tell us which artistic styles were fashionable, what kind of people were deemed important, and how those people wished to be remembered. Private collections and public exhibitions of portraits can go even farther in demonstrating how our conception of history changes over time. This exhibition of nineteenth-century portraits from the Pennsylvania Academy features paintings acquired over the past two hundred years for a variety of reasons. Most of the artists and sitters are well known, but a few remain anonymous. Some are remembered for their historical importance and others because they were so ordinary, that is, typical of their class or profession.

Although most of the portraits in the collection of the Pennsylvania Academy were painted by academically trained artists, there are also fine examples of plain-style portraits produced by self-taught limners. It is important to recognize that these plain portraits were often based on the fancier, European-derived work of artists such as Charles Willson Peale (see cat. no. 6), Gilbert Stuart (see cat. nos. 1-3), and Thomas Sully (see cat. nos. 12, 16, and 29). Working in Philadelphia at the end of the eighteenth century and the beginning of the nineteenth, these men helped to establish that city as America's first artistic center; and their art served as fashionable models of style for other portraitists. Philadelphia, the nation's capital from 1790 to 1800, brought together numerous politicians, military figures, scientists, intellectuals, and artists to form a richly varied cultural community that fueled the portrait-painting trade.

This brief essay focuses on the origins of the portrait trade in Philadelphia with special reference to works in the collection of the Pennsylvania Academy of the Fine Arts. These portraits represent not only the specific interests of Philadelphians but, in many respects, those of the nation as a whole. Organized in 1805, the Pennsylvania Academy was concerned with the creation of a national artistic identity, the edification of the American people through the study of art, and the promotion of native-born artists. Portraiture was the most accessible form of art that fulfilled these goals. Charles Willson Peale, one of the Pennsylvania Academy's founders, had already established the first public gallery in the United States—a museum that included many of his portraits of military and political figures. Located on the second floor of the State House (now Independence Hall), Peale's museum had semiofficial status by virtue of its site and function. As shown in his monumental self-portrait *The Artist in His Museum* (fig. 1), Peale hung portraits of notable Americans above display cases filled with stuffed birds, insects, minerals, and fossils. The placement of his portraits above these natural specimens was meant to impress the museum visitor with the order of the evolutionary process, or what was then called the "great chain of being."[1]

The Artist in His Museum combined scientific ideas drawn from the Enlightenment of the eighteenth century and a much older aesthetic tradition linked to the function of the portrait. From ancient times, public portraiture was a means of promoting civic virtue and dynastic legitimacy. Roman military and political figures were often depicted as sculpted figures in round frames, known as *imagines clipeatae* or shield portraits. Along with ancestor portraits, these shield portraits were held in reverence in the Roman household. Peale's presentation of his portraits in gilded oval frames was a kind of secularization of the ancient form of ancestor worship. In the nineteenth century, the use of such imagery derived from the classical past was most often associated with portraits of George Washington and

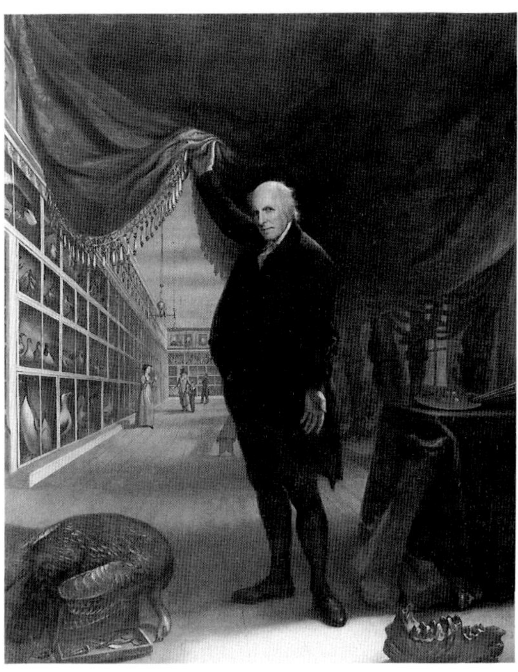

Fig. 1
Charles Willson Peale (1741–1827)
The Artist in His Museum, 1822
Pennsylvania Academy of the Fine Arts, Gift of Mrs. Sarah Harrison (The Joseph Harrison, Jr. Collection) 1878.1.2

other political figures.[2] Classicism, the use of forms modeled after ancient Greek and Roman art, is certainly the most distinctive iconographic and stylistic feature of Rembrandt Peale's best-known portrait of George Washington (fig. 2). The son of Charles Willson Peale, Rembrandt (see cat. no. 30) drew on ideas that were only implicit in his father's portraits. The Washington portrait was based on a study from life (1795, Historical Society of Pennsylvania, Philadelphia), but it is distinguished by the trompe l'oeil (fools the eye) painted frame derived directly from classical sources. A head of Jupiter fills the keystone; oak leaves, an ancient symbol of honor, surround Washington's bust; and the Latin inscription *Patriae Pater* (Father of the Country) graces the plinth supporting the oval portrait.[3]

Like his predecessor Gilbert Stuart, Rembrandt Peale hoped to earn fame and fortune by painting numerous replicas of his Washington portrait for both public and private consumption. In the 1830s, he sold one replica to the United States government and sent another on tour in Europe. During this period, Peale's "Porthole Washington" (as it became known) began to rival Stuart's earlier portrait of Washington, called the Athenaeum head (cat. no. 1) for government recognition as the official likeness of the first president. Both artists produced over sixty replicas of their respective portraits of Washington; and Peale copied Stuart's, as well. The Pennsylvania Academy owns three of Peale's copies, two Athenaeum

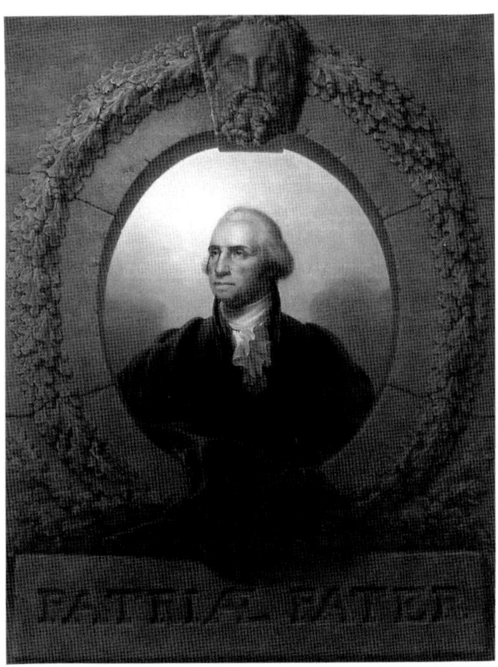

Fig. 2
Rembrandt Peale (1778–1860)
George Washington, Patriae Pater, ca. 1824
Pennsylvania Academy of the Fine Arts, Bequest of Mrs. Sarah Harrison (The Joseph Harrison, Jr. Collection), 1912.14.4

heads and another referred to as the Vaughn type. Although today uniqueness and originality are the most prized elements in a work of art, more intangible qualities, such as "nobility" and "grand effect," were held in high esteem during the nineteenth century. It made little difference to viewers whether they were looking at an original portrait or a replica by the same artist. It was the identity of the sitter and his or her importance that gave value and meaning to the work. Portraitists like the Peales and Stuart rose in stature in accordance with the fame of their sitters.

During the first three decades of the nineteenth century, several Philadelphia publishers sought to capitalize on the popular demand for images of famous Americans. *Delaplaine's Repository of the Lives and Portraits of Distinguished American Characters*, which appeared between 1815 and 1818, included both images and biographies of notable men. Modeled on the Greek and Roman practice of composing biographies of public heroes, this publication claimed that its illustrations of portraits gave it special relevance to contemporary American audiences. Despite the presence of portraits by numerous well-known portrait painters, among them Charles Willson Peale and Benjamin West, this ambitious project was a financial failure. Two other publications with portrait engravings were more successful: *Biographies of the Signers of the Declaration of Independence* by John Sanderson

(Philadelphia, 1820-27) and *Acting American Theatre*, edited by Mathias Lopez and Francis C. Wemyss (Philadelphia, 1826).

The most popular of these biographical compendia, however, proved to be the four-volume *National Portrait Gallery of Distinguished Americans*, published in Philadelphia by James Herring and James B. Longacre between 1834 and 1839.[4] It contains engravings by fifty different artists, including Gilbert Stuart, Thomas Sully, and Henry Inman (see cat. nos. 24 and 27). The aim of the book was to produce a patriotic assemblage of portraits that would constitute "a monument of national gratitude and the evidence of a just appreciation of the brave, the honorable, and virtuous achievements which indicate to the world the high destiny of the republic."[5]

The original portraits on which the prints were based came from both private and public collections. Over the years, the Pennsylvania Academy of the Fine Arts has acquired four of the images illustrated in this publication: David Martin's *Benjamin Franklin* (1767, a replica of the version in the White House, Washington, D. C.), Henry Sargent's *Benjamin Lincoln* (ca. 1806, replica of the version in the Massachusetts Historical Society, Boston), Thomas Sully's *John McLean* (1831); and John Wesley Jarvis's *William Harris Crawford* (1823, cat. no. 19). Crawford's biography was typical of those included in the publication. It described at length his early years, his political achievements in Washington, and his straightforward personality, characterized by "modest virtue, sound sense, and stern integrity," ideal qualities sought after in a politician.[6]

The art of the early nineteenth century in Europe and the United States was marked not only by the revival of interest in ancient forms, known as neoclassicism, but also by romanticism. Each style was deemed appropriate for a specific type of portraiture, which depended on the occupation of the sitter. Political figures were often painted in neoclassical style; theatrical personalities were usually depicted in a more romantic mode. During the federal period, Philadelphia became a leading theater center; and Thomas Sully, the city's most prolific portrait painter, was one of the artists who introduced theatrical subjects to the American public.[7] His romantic style of painting, which relied on dramatic poses, exaggerated facial expressions, and backdrops with swirling clouds or historical settings, served well to convey the sitter's theatrical role. Sully's portrait of a famous British actor, *George Frederick Cooke as Richard III* (cat. no. 12), was one of the first works of art acquired for the permanent collection of the Pennsylvania Academy and a perennial favorite in the annual exhibitions. The Shakespearean theme and medieval setting elevated the image from mere portraiture to the realm of history painting.

European art academies had long ranked history painting higher than portraiture in the hierarchy of subject matter.[8] Because its subjects were drawn from notable historical events and famous works of literature, history painting was thought to require greater artistic skill and academic learning than portraiture. Such subjects were intended to be morally uplifting and to instill in viewers a sense of valor and civic virtue. In the United States, however, where the choice of subject was more often governed by popular taste than by strict academic rules, portraiture had always been more popular. Portrait painting, nevertheless, absorbed academic principles of theory and design and, to some degree, the moral function of history painting. The panoply of portraits displayed in Peale's museum, for example, represented one of the earliest attempts to record the history and moral rectitude of the United States through the faces of its national heroes.

As American society changed in the nineteenth century, portrait painters began to expand their vocabulary of style, poses, and props to meet its new demands. Patronage became more broadly based. The demand increased for public portraits of America's new political elite. There was also an interest in sophisticated paintings that suggested more than the mere likeness of the sitter. Although principally a portraitist, Thomas Sully also painted what he called "fancy pieces," which bridged the gap between history painting and portraiture. These were often subjects of his own invention: theatrical or literary scenes and sentimental images of young children. Romantic in conception, these images transported the viewer from the everyday world to the realm of imagination through the use of costumes and props. Sully's portrait of George Frederick Cooke was one of the earliest of these fancy pieces, and it established a taste for romantic portraiture in Philadelphia. Both Sully and his son-in-law and student, John Neagle (see cat. nos. 21 and 26), went on to paint numerous theatrical portraits in the 1820s and 1830s. Several were acquired for the Pennsylvania Academy's permanent collection, among them portraits of Charles and Frances Anne (Fanny) Kemble, Edmund Kean, and William Macready—all celebrated British actors who were popular performers on the Philadelphia stage during this period. For the most part, however, the people who provided the patronage necessary to sustain the careers of American portrait painters in the early nineteenth century were not celebrities. They were usually prosperous, middle- or upper-class educated, and socially conscious, citizens who wanted their likenesses painted as family records, not necessarily for public display. Most of the more than two thousand portraits painted by Sully, for example, fall into this category. Sully kept a detailed account book in which he recorded the sitter's name, the size of the portrait, the amount of time it took to paint, and the fee.[9] His fees, like those of most portrait painters, were based on the size of the portrait, which included head only, bust, "kit-kat" (between bust and three-quarter-length), two sizes of half-length, and full-length. In 1837, at the height of his long career, Sully charged two hundred dollars for a bust and a thousand dollars for a full-length portrait. Between 1810 and 1850, his prices rose steadily, although not dramatically; and he was able to maintain a large family and a studio in a comfortable townhouse on fashionable Fifth Street in Philadelphia. But Sully was by no means a wealthy man. In order to finance a trip to England in 1837 to paint the young Queen Victoria, he needed an advance from his patron, the Society of the Sons of Saint George, as well as orders from several Philadelphia collectors to paint copies of old-master paintings.

The competition among Philadelphia portrait painters was especially keen in the 1830s. The exhibitions of the Artists' Fund Society during this decade were organized as a concerted effort to promote their work over that of artists from outside the city, particularly from New York. Established in 1824 to encourage local support for living American artists, the Artists' Fund Society counted among its members several noted portraitists, including Thomas Sully and John Neagle.[10] Controversy involving two portraits (cat. nos. 26 and 27) shown in the Artists' Fund Society exhibition of 1837 seems to suggest that, among critics at least, there was a tacit recognition of a Philadelphia portrait style distinct from that practiced by artists in New York or Boston. It was a style characterized by loose brushwork, brilliant coloring, and romantic backgrounds filled with swirling clouds and billowing drapery.

This Philadelphia style had its American roots in the art of Gilbert Stuart but was nurtured by British portraiture of the late eighteenth and early nineteenth centuries, especially the works of Thomas Gainsborough and Sir Thomas Lawrence. In his memoirs, Thomas Sully recalled his early comparison of Gainsborough and Stuart during a trip to London in 1809: "The manner of Gainsborough struck me as being, in its result, very similar to Stuart's; only that Stuart's general practice is firmer in the handling. . .and although on inspection the work seemed rugged, smeared, and scratched; yet at a moderate distance, it appeared to me to be more like nature than any picture in the room." Later, during his 1837 visit to London, Sully was even more impressed by Lawrence: "The elements of Lawrence's style are Dignity, Elegance, and taste," characteristics that describe Sully's work, as well.[11]

The portrait style of Henry Inman (see cat. nos. 24 and 27), especially during his years in Philadelphia, from 1831 to 1834, was also influenced by this prevailing romantic mode that stemmed from British art.[12] Increased contact with works by both Sully and Neagle, whom he admired, may have prompted Inman to apply his paints more freely and to heighten contrasts of light and dark. Like these other artists, Inman manifested his romantic sensibility in literary and theatrical subjects, such as his *Macready in the Character of William Tell* (ca. 1827, Metropolitan Museum of Art, New York). Inman produced drawings and paintings based on popular romantic novels by Washington Irving and James Fenimore Cooper, as well.[13]

In addition to the romantic, English-inspired, painterly approach of Sully, Neagle, and Inman, a linear style of painting remained popular in Philadelphia during the first half of the nineteenth century. This linear style, which can be traced to the colonial period, is most evident in the work of Charles Willson Peale and his family. In Peale's portraits, the carefully drawn details of the face and clothes, fully modeled with light and shade, often contrast markedly with the simplicity of the background. Ironically, Peale's academic style, based on his studies with Benjamin West in London (see cat. no. 8), may have had its greatest impact on the art of self-taught limners (see cat. nos. 9 and 11). They often emulated the sharpness of his drawing, the clarity of his forms, and his use of traditional poses.

Conscious variations in style were employed by plain painters, as well as academic portraitists. The itinerant painter William Matthew Prior (1806-1873) was capable of painting fully modeled faces or simple, linear ones with no shading—depending on the aesthetic taste and the pocketbook of his clients. An advertisement for his work in the *Maine Inquirer* (April 5, 1831) stated: "Persons wishing for a flat picture can have a likeness without shade or shadow at one quarter the price." His rate for one of these quick, tempera "flat pictures," measuring 16½ by 12½ inches, was $2.92, including frame and glass.[14] Such simple portraits could have been afforded even by the working classes of the period. In 1830, for example, the average daily wage for an artisan in Philadelphia was $1.73.

The linear approach to academic portrait painting underwent further modification when it came into contact with French neoclassical painting. Rembrandt Peale, after two trips to France between 1808 and 1810, combined aspects of his father's rather old-fashioned linear style with the more up-to-date features of neoclassicism. His style of painting, with its hard, porcelain-like finish, strong highlights, and sculptural modeling of forms (see cat. no. 30) was quite distinct from that of Sully, a difference readily perceived at the time. John Neal, a well-known writer of the period who at one time was said to have been in love with Rembrandt Peale's daughter, Rosalba, provided characterizations of several American portrait painters in his autobiographical novel, *Randolph*. About the stylistic diffences between Thomas Sully and Rembrandt Peale, he wrote, "I should prefer Mr. Sully, I think, to any other artist that I have known, if I wanted the portrait of a youthful, passionate, enthusiast, male or female;—but, if I wanted the likeness of a sober-minded man or woman, I would go to Mr. Peale."[15]

With the introduction of photography to Philadelphia in 1839, the issues of likeness and style became infinitely more complex for the portrait painter. The camera was capable of capturing a more accurate likeness than any portrait painter could; and it could do it more quickly and at less expense. By the 1850s, a cheap daguerreotype cost as little as twenty-five cents, although hand-painted, imperial-sized photographs of celebrities ran as high as five hundred dollars.[16] But this also meant that the painted portrait once again became the domain of the rich. When almost everyone could afford a daguerreotype, the social status associated with owning a painted portrait increased. In the mid-nineteenth century, while there seems to have been a decline in the portrait trade as a whole,[17] there was a tendency for painters to focus more attention on sitters with celebrity status. The careers of artists such as George P. A. Healy (see cat. no. 31) and James R. Lambdin (see cat. no. 37) were based primarily on images of famous people and depended on official, rather than private, patronage. Portrait painters, like Thomas Sully, who kept their old middle-class clientele were often forced to reduce the prices of their portraits and increase their output.[18]

Photography affected the aesthetics as well as the economics of portrait painting in nineteenth-century America. Its impact was two-fold and contradictory: while some artists were encouraged to produce even more realistic portraits, others were liberated from the confines of verisimilitude. Thomas Eakins's quest for penetrating, psychological expression in his portraits was certainly enhanced by his use of photography in the 1880s and early 1890s. A great admirer of the poet Walt Whitman, Eakins kept photographs of the aging bard tacked to his studio wall even after he finished painting a portrait of him in 1888 (fig. 3).[19] Whitman shared Eakins's love of realistic detail, especially when it revealed the personality of the sitter. About his own portrait by Eakins, Whitman said; "It is a portrait of power and realism ('a poor, old, blind, despised and dying king')."[20] But this truthfulness in Eakins's images was not appreciated by all of his sitters. In 1913, when he gave his portrait by Eakins (cat. no. 43) to the Pennsylvania Academy, Charles Edmund Dana wrote, "I trust you will do justice to my absolute lack of personal vanity in permitting myself to go down to posterity in so unpleasant a presentment."[21]

Eakins's entire career as a portrait painter was marked by a singular lack of traditional patronage. There were no fashionable beauties or famous politicians among his sitters; instead, he concentrated his efforts on family, friends, and students. In discussing Eakins's place among late nineteenth-century portraitists, the critic Samuel Isham clearly expressed the contemporary taste for more elegance and refinement in portraiture: "No one would wish his sitters more modishly clad or more self-conscious. Their interest lies in their personality, and that is excellently given. The drawing is the most searching and delicate, the figures are well constructed and stand with notable firmness of their feet, and every line of

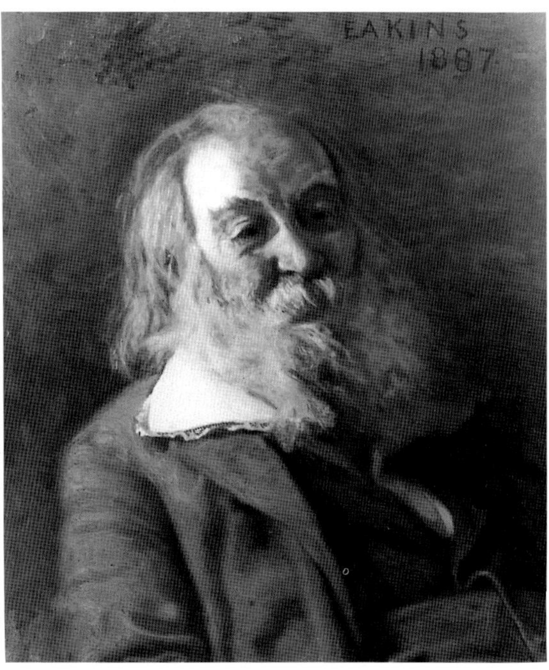

Fig. 3
THOMAS EAKINS (1884–1916)
WALT WHITMAN, 1888
Pennsylvania Academy of the Fine Arts, General Fund, 1917.1

face and raiment has character. The artist seems to say: 'Here is the man, what more do you want?' but the paint is apt to be laid on inelegantly. There are vast expanses of background that are thin or dry or muddy or cold. The eye longs for beauty of surface, richness of impasto or transparent depths of shadow."[22]

Those artists who did depend on a wealthy and socially prominent clientele often avoided realism and adopted instead a dazzling, painterly style that was suited to the display of sumptuous fabrics and elegant poses. Artists such as John Singer Sargent (see cat. no. 38), Cecilia Beaux (see cat. no. 39), and William Merritt Chase (see cat. no. 41) established their reputations as portrait painters among an increasingly sophisticated set of international patrons. Isham considered Beaux's work the epitome of modernism. Not only were her portraits elegant in style, but they also captured a sense of immediacy and liveliness that Isham found lacking in Sargent's work. "She is in sympathy with her sitters, and they are likable and charming and enlist the affections of the spectator as those of Sargent rarely do after they get beyond the age of eight or ten."[23]

By the end of the nineteenth century, the Pennsylvania Academy had instituted special classes devoted to portrait painting. The first, taught by Thomas Eakins, is recorded in the school catalogue for 1881/82. It was offered three times each week in three-hour sessions, along with cast and life drawing and anatomy lessons. The anatomy lessons were augmented by a series of lectures on specific parts of the body. According to the catalogue: "[There were two lectures] devoted to the muscles of the face and the anatomy of expression, both in man and the lower animals. Four lectures to the eye, nose, mouth, chin, and ear. Two lectures to the skin, with its various wrinkles (especially those of the face), and the subcutaneous layer of fat and the blood vessels in the superficial fascia. One lecture to the hair and beard, and postural expression."[24] The scientific approach to the rendering of human form suggested by this detailed description mirrors Eakins's own realistic approach to portraiture.

After Eakins left the Pennsylvania Academy in 1886, his realist style was emulated, although never surpassed, in paintings by Bernard Uhle (1847-1930), who became the first Academy instructor to specialize in teaching portrait painting. He was followed in the 1890s by Robert Vonnoh (see cat. no. 40), Cecilia Beaux, and William Merritt Chase, artists who took a different approach to portraiture. Their style of painting, with loosely handled paint surface, idealized facial features, and greater emphasis on elegance, achieved great popularity during this decade. Under their direction, the Pennsylvania Academy's portrait course proved so popular that it was divided into two sections, one devoted to the drawing and painting of the head and the other to the figure as a whole. By 1900, a section for advanced students was added. Beaux and another Academy graduate, Hugh H. Breckenridge (1870-1937), taught the sections devoted to the head; Chase taught the figure and advanced portrait classes.

Portraits by Cecilia Beaux, Robert Vonnoh, and William Merritt Chase, although usually privately commissioned, were often shown publicly in the annual exhibitions at the Pennsylvania Academy. Judging from the number of prizes won by these portraits and the praise they received, their success was second only to that of impressionist landscape paintings.[25] In 1891 and 1892, for example, Beaux won the Mary Smith Prize for the best work by a woman artist for her portraiture. She also won the Temple Gold Medal in 1900 for *Mother and Daughter*, a portrait of Mrs. Clement A. Griscom and her daughter Frances (1898, Pennsylvania Academy of the Fine Arts, see fig. 4). Although most of Beaux's portraits were privately commissioned, they had great popular appeal because they not only represented the sitters as individuals but also could be viewed as typologies of a certain social class or gender role.[26] With titles such as *New England Woman* (1895, Pennsylvania Academy of the Fine Arts), *Mother and Daughter*, and *A Little Girl* (cat. no. 39), Beaux sought to broaden the audience for her imagery. Rather than painting mere likenesses of specific people, she was representing generic types: the stoic Yankee, the society belle, and the innocent child.[27]

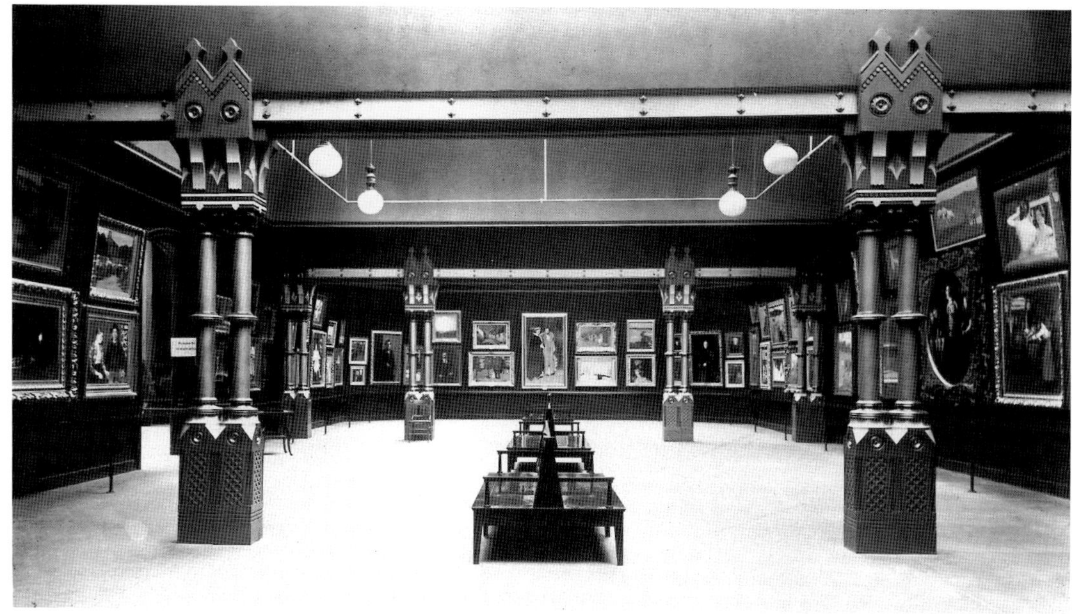

Fig. 4
View of the 1900 annual exhibition
at the Pennsylvania Academy (Pennsylvania Academy Archives),
showing the prominent position given to Cecilia Beaux's portrait
Mother and Daughter (center of photograph).

George de Forest Brush's *Mother and Child* (cat. no. 42) is another example of the kind of typological portraiture that found a ready audience during this period.[28] The artist established his career with a series of popular portraits of his wife and children based on traditional images of the Madonna and Christ Child, several of which were exhibited at the Pennsylvania Academy in the late 1890s. One was awarded the Academy's Temple Gold Medal in 1897; and, the following year, another was featured in the center of the gallery, a prominent position reserved for the most highly praised work. The response of one critic, writing for *Century Magazine*, expresses the contemporary attitude toward Brush's idealized portraits of modern motherhood: "The picture suggests no Italian school or painter, yet reminds us of the Italian conception. The forms are modern, living people of to-day, while the sympathetic feeling is ancient, common to all lofty art. Local truths of likeness are apparent . . . but above these we feel the universal truths of maternal tenderness and infantile grace."[29]

Many scholars today have suggested that such a conception of family and female gender roles represents not a universal truth but one grounded in the specific social needs and historical conditions of the late nineteenth century.[30] At a time when family structure was increasingly under attack from industrialization and urbanization, conservative artists like Brush maintained the illusion of permanence and social harmony with images of the ideal American family couched in the visual language of Renaissance art.

Although portraits were routinely included in the annual exhibitions at the Pennsylvania Academy, it was not until 1887 that the Academy organized a special show devoted solely to historical portraiture. This massive exhibition of over five hundred colonial and early nineteenth-century portraits was the first of its kind in the nation.[31] Among the forty-six works drawn from the Pennsylvania Academy's permanent collection were Gilbert Stuart's portraits of Mr. and Mrs. George Plumstead (cat. nos. 2 and 3), Thomas Sully's *George Frederick Cooke as Richard III*, Henry Inman's sketch of Sully (cat. no. 27), and Samuel Bell Waugh's *Cope Brothers* (cat. no. 33). Lenders to the exhibition included both individuals and institutions in the Philadelphia area, such as the American Philosophical Society and the Historical Society of Pennsylvania.

In conception, the exhibition was modeled on published editions of historical portraits, such as the previously mentioned *National Portrait Gallery of Distinguished Americans*. Although there were a few works by unidentified artists of unidentified sitters, most of the subjects and the painters were well known. There were nine portraits of George Washington, more than of any other sitter. They included each of Stuart's famous images: the Athenaeum head, a version of the full-length Lansdowne portrait (executed in 1796 and acquired by the Pennsylvania Academy of the Fine Arts in 1811), and the original version of the Vaughn portrait (1795, National Gallery of Art, Washington, D. C.). In addition, there were three portraits of Washington by Charles Willson Peale, two by Joseph Wright (1756-1793), and one by Adolph Wertmüller (1751-1811). The catalogue, arranged alphabetically by sitter, provided a brief biography for each artist but paid little attention to matters of style or attribution. This emphasis on the fame of the sitter, rather than the artist, links the exhibition to the classical tradition of portraiture. The writer of the catalogue thanked the lenders for the "denuding of their walls of their most precious household treasures—their very *lares* and *penates* [the gods who watched over the house in ancient times]." During the 1880s and 1890s, at the height of the American Renaissance, such overt references to classicism were common and very fashionable.

The next special exhibition of portraits at the Pennsylvania Academy, held in 1893, was devoted to colonial portrait prints. It included 275 mezzotints and engravings, all drawn from a single private collection;[32] and it marked a shift in the practice of collecting portraits. Previously, large collections of historical portraits had been amassed primarily by institutions; but in the 1890s, private collectors also started to buy historical portraits. In 1899, Thomas B. Clarke, a noted collector of American landscapes and genre paintings, began buying early American portraits because they were relatively inexpensive.[33] When his portrait collection was offered for sale in 1919, the catalogue claimed that "a collection of canvases of this character has not before been offered to the public." It went on to note that "every museum in the country has gone forth during the past few years toward acquiring early American portraits."[34] Indeed, many of the portraits from the Clarke sale found their way into both private and public collections. For example, another avid portrait collector, Henry E. Huntington, better known for his interest in eighteenth-century British portraiture, purchased several works for his newly established showpiece of British and American culture, the Huntington Library, in San Marino, California.

Clarke's portrait collection was not completely dispersed with the 1919 sale. In 1928, the Philadelphia Museum of Art showed 164 portraits from his collection; and the museum's director, Fiske Kimball, took special pleasure in noting that "it is a matter of more than local interest that so many of the pictures were painted in Philadelphia, so long the metropolis and capital of this country, and that thirty-six are known to have been painted in Pennsylvania."[35]

The 1920s proved to be an especially active decade for the exhibiting and collecting of American portraits at the Pennsylvania Academy, due primarily to the efforts of John Frederick Lewis. He served as president of the Academy for twenty-five years, from 1907 to 1932. During that time, the portrait exhibitions began to focus on artists rather than sitters. Under Lewis's aegis, the Pennsylvania Academy mounted shows devoted to Cecilia Beaux (1907), Thomas Eakins (1917), Thomas Sully (1922), the Peale family (1923), and John Neagle (1925). Lewis was a maritime lawyer by profession and an art collector by avocation. In addition to American historical portraits, he collected title pages, portrait engravings, Babylonian and Assyrian clay tablets, and Indo-Persian watercolors and illuminated manuscripts. His diverse taste in art helps account for the nature of his interest in portraits.

From an old and socially prominent Philadelphia family, Lewis was well acquainted with the American portrait tradition. Portraits of his grandparents had been painted by Jacob Eichholtz in 1827; and these, along with over two hundred portraits from his collection were given to the Pennsylvania Academy in 1933.[36] As a collector, he was especially interested in local portrait painters and set out to gather together works by members of the Peale family, Thomas Sully, Bass Otis (1784-1861), and John Neagle. Connoisseurship was not of primary importance to Lewis, however. In 1934, when the Pennsylvania Academy exhibited the newly acquired Lewis collection, Mantle Fielding noted in his introduction to the catalogue that many of the attributions were based on records of ownership and not on scholarship.[37] Fortunately, another authority on early American portraiture, William Sawitsky, annotated a copy of the catalogue with remarks on the misidentification of sitters and the doubtful attributions.[38] Because Sawitisky was more attuned to the issue of copies and replicas in American portraiture, his observations have proven helpful in correctly identifying many of these portraits.

Several works in the current exhibition, especially those by self-taught artists (cat. nos. 4, 5, 11, and 14), demonstrate that Lewis was attracted to both the plain and the academic styles of portrait painting. He was primarily interested in the historical value of the collection and hoped that Americans would begin to appreciate their national school of portraiture: "The citizens of the United States do not recognize the fact that their country is a nation and has an art history of its own, which will become more precious every year, and which has its archaic examples just like the English school, the French school or the early Italian schools. Examples of this early art will become every year more valuable and likewise more sought after by the different art institutions of the country."[39] Lewis's appreciation of "archaic," or what we now term "plain," painting was one of the earliest attempts to promote this style in American art.[40]

Perhaps the most visible legacy of this wave of portrait collecting that began at the turn of the century was the movement to establish a national portrait gallery in the United States. The idea stemmed from a nineteenth-century phenomenon—the formation of government-sponsored museums. The first such public portrait museum was the National Portrait Gallery in London, organized in 1856 to house a "national pantheon" of British citizens. In an address to Parliament, Lord Palmerston described its function as "an incentive to mental exertion, to noble action, to good conduct."[41] The Victorian sensibility behind this endeavor was also a motivating factor in the organization of two important portrait exhibitions at the Pennsylvania Academy, which can be considered precursors of the founding of a national gallery in this country.

The first of these exhibitions was held in 1905 to celebrate the centennial of the Pennsylvania Academy. The show was called the *Gallery of National Portraiture* because, according to newpaper accounts of the day, it was intended to spur interest in the formation of a permanent installation of portraiture.[42] Among the 140 works on display were examples of both historical and contemporary portraits from the Pennsylvania Academy's collection and from private and public lenders. Most reviews of the exhibition expressed a preference for the historical portraits, especially the work of Gilbert Stuart and Henry Inman: "The exhibition affords a series of lessons to portrait painters, who would do well to study it closely. These old painters did not depend on picturesque dresses of the day for the charm their work contains. Abstract all that, and one finds a power in the simplicity of the composition and the direct, workman like style of execution."[43] This interest in historical portraits led to the organization of another exhibition at the time of the sesquicentennial of the Declaration of Independence, in 1926. That exhibition, entitled *A Gallery of National Portraiture and Historic Scenes,* placed emphasis on the work of early nineteenth-century Philadelphia portraitists who had strong ties to the Pennsylvania Academy. The brochure, written by John Frederick Lewis, explained why the Academy was the most fitting venue for this ambitious loan exhibition: it was the oldest art institution in the United States and among its founders were several men who had played an important role in the early politics of this country. Of the 426 works in the catalogue, many were from the Pennsylvania Academy's permanent collection. These included paintings by Gilbert Stuart, Thomas Sully, Benjamin West, William Jennys (see cat. nos. 4 and 5), and George P. A. Healy that are in the present exhibition. Although the show included the work of late nineteenth-century painters, as well—among them, Samuel Bell Waugh, Thomas Eakins, and John Singer Sargent—its greatest impact was in the area of historical portraits. These images still elicited a patriotic, rather than aesthetic, response: "If one is to derive from the exhibition the greatest degree of pleasure, he must approach it as an American citizen and not as a critic of art."[44]

It was not until 1962 that the United States government capitalized on this patriotic impulse. In that year, Congress voted to establish a national museum in Washington, D. C., devoted to American portraits of men and women who have made significant contributions to this country.[45] The National Portrait Gallery now collects both historical and contemporary paintings and sculpture, as well as prints, drawings, and photographs. Like its nineteenth-century precursors, the National Portrait Gallery organizes exhibitions devoted to famous sitters, but it also focuses on the work of individual portrait painters. Its scholarly catalogues on portraiture have contributed greatly to our knowledge of the individual styles and commercial practices of artists such as Charles Willson Peale, Gilbert Stuart, Thomas Sully, and Henry Inman.

The research generated by the National Portrait Gallery has in turn brought renewed attention to the strengths of the Pennsylvania Academy's portrait collection. Among the most rewarding aspects of recent scholarship in the field of American art have been iconographic studies on the work of Charles Willson Peale.[46] Future studies of the collection no doubt will produce new insights into the diversity and social relevance of other artists' work, as well. There is a need for more in-depth studies of patronage and of differences between images made for private satisfaction and those intended for public display. Such studies can provide new information about the social aspirations and cultural ambitions of sitters and should serve as models for similar analyses of nineteenth-century artists, such as Thomas Sully and John Neagle. Finally, the field of gender studies has also yielded new perspectives on the social roles represented in nineteenth-century portraits of men, women, and children.[47]

The following catalogue reveals the rich variety of portrait types in the collection of the Pennsylvania Academy of the Fine Arts and touches briefly on the compelling aesthetic and social issues that are suggested by these images. It is hoped that the catalogue and the exhibition will stimulate further research on the meaning of specific works, the social role of portraiture, and the economics of the portrait business and, in so doing, will reanimate these faces from the past and provide us with a fuller understanding of our history.

•

Notes

1 Roger B. Stein, "Charles Willson Peale's Expressive Design, *The Artist in his Museum*," in *New Perspectives on Charles Willson Peale* (Pittsburgh: University of Pittsburgh Press, 1991), pp. 167-218.

2 For a lengthier discussion, see *The Classical Spirit in American Portraiture*, exhib. cat. (Providence: Brown University, 1976).

3 Carol Hevner, *Rembrandt Peale*, 1778-1860, *A Life in the Arts*, exhib. cat. (Philadelphia: Historical Society of Pennsylvania, 1985), no. 66.

4 For a discussion of the portraits reproduced in this work, see Robert Stuart, *A Nineteenth-Century Gallery of Distinguished Americans*, exhib. cat. (Washington, D. C.: National Portrait Gallery, 1969), pp. 5-9.

5 Herring and Longacre (1839), vol. 4, p. 2.

6 Herring and Longacre (1839), vol. 4, p. 3.

7 For a discussion of the history of American theatrical portraits, see Monroe H. Fabian, *Portraits of the American Stage*, 1771-1971, exhib. cat. (Washington, D. C.: National Portrait Gallery, 1971).

8 For a further discussion of these academic hierarchies, see Sir Joshua Reynolds, *Discourses on Art*, ed. Robert Wark (San Marino, Calif.: Huntington Library and Art Gallery, 1959).

9 Sully's register is in the collection of the Historical Society of Pennsylvania. The artist also listed his prices in a manuscript entitled "Hints for Pictures," which has entries from 1809 to 1871, Yale University Library, New Haven. For a further discussion of Sully's career, see Monroe H. Fabian, *Mr. Sully, Portrait Painter, The Works of Thomas Sully* 1783-1872, exhib. cat. (Washington, D. C.: National Portrait Gallery, 1983), pp. 10-24.

10 For further discussion of the Artists' Fund Society, see Ellen Wood Ramsey, "The Artists' Fund Society of Philadelphia, 1835-1845" (unpublished master's thesis, University of Iowa, 1990); and Robert W. Torchia, *John Neagle, Philadelphia Portrait Painter*, exhib. cat. (Philadelphia: Historical Society of Pennsylvania, 1989), pp. 58-70.

11 "Memoirs of the professional life of Thomas Sully, Dedicated to his brother artists." Nov. 1851, Henry Francis Du Pont Winterthur Museum, Delaware. This manuscript appears to be a preliminary of *Hints to Young Painters and the Process of Portrait Painting as practiced by the late Thomas Sully* (Philadelphia: J. M. Stoddart and Co., 1873). The Winterthur manuscript, however, includes more art criticism, some of which is repeated in John Neagle's notebooks in the collection of the Historical Society of Pennsylvania.

12 Theodore Bolton, "Henry Inman, An Account of his Life and Work," *Art Quarterly* 3 (Autumn 1940), pp. 353-373. Bolton termed Inman's style "Romantic Realism" to distinguish it from the work of Stuart and Sully, whom he saw as more idealizing in their approach to portraiture.

13 For examples, see William H. Gerdts and Carrie Rebora, *The Art of Henry Inman*, exhib. cat. (Washington, D. C.: National Portrait Gallery, 1987).

14 Nina Fletcher Little, "William M. Prior, Traveling Artist," *Antiques* 53 (Jan. 1948), pp. 44-48.

15 John Neal, *Randolph* (Baltimore: 1823), pp. 68-69.

16 Barbara McCandless, "The Portrait Studio and the Celebrity," in *Photography in Nineteenth-Century America*, exhib. cat. (Fort Worth: Amon Carter Museum, 1991), p. 58.

17 Theodore Bolton, "Charles Loring Elliot, An Account of His Life and Work," *Art Quarterly* 5 (Winter 1942), p. 61.

18 Fabian (1983), p. 17.

19 Several photographs of Whitman are visible in a view of Eakins's studio taken about 1891-92, when the sculptor William O'Donovan (1844-1920) was there working on a bust of the poet. Although Eakins was active as a photographer, he probably did not take all of these images. For further discussion, see Carolyn Kinder Carr, "A Friendship and a Photograph: Sophia Williams, Talcott Williams, and Walt Whitman," *American Art Journal* 21, no. 1 (1989), pp. 2-12; and William Innes Homer, "Who Took Eakins' Photographs?" *Artnews* 82 (May 1983), pp. 112-119.

20 Quoted in Lloyd Goodrich, *Thomas Eakins* (Cambridge, Mass.: Harvard University Press, 1982), vol. 2, p. 34.

21 Dana to John F. Lewis, June 23, 1913, Correspondence, Board Presidents, Pennsylvania Academy Archives.

22 Samuel Isham, *The History of American Painting* (New York: Macmillan and Co., 1936), pp. 525-526

23 Isham (1936), p. 530.

24 *Circular of the Committee on Instruction* (Philadelphia: Pennsylvania Academy of the Fine Arts, 1881), p. 10.

25 For a discussion of the rise of impressionism at the Pennsylvania Academy, see Susan Danly, *Light, Air, and Color: American Impressionist Paintings from the Collection of the Pennsylvania Academy of the Fine Arts*, exhib. cat. (Philadelphia: Pennsylvania Academy of the Fine Arts, 1990), pp. 11-23.

26 For further discussion of typologies in images of American women, see Martha Banta, *Imaging American Women, Idea and Ideas in Cultural History* (New York: Columbia University Press, 1987), pp. 377-390.

27 For further discussion of typology in Beaux's work, see Tara Tappert, "Choices—The Life and Career of Cecilia Beaux: A Professional Biography," Ph.D. diss., George Washington University, 1990, pp. 299-390.

28 For a contemporary discussion of the Madonna and Child type in Brush's work, see Harrison S. Morris, "American Portraiture of Children," *Scribner's Magazine* 30 (Dec. 1901), pp. 641-656.

29 "George de Forest Brush's Mother and Child," *Century Magazine* 29 (April 1896), pp. 954.

30 Jane Collier et al., "Is There a Family? New Anthropological Views," in *Rethinking the Family*, ed. Barrie Thorne with Marilyn Yalom (New York: Longhorn, 1982), pp. 25-39.

31 *Loan Exhibition of Historical Portraits*, exhib. cat. (Philadelphia: Pennsylvania Academy of the Fine Arts, 1887), p. 3. The introduction to this catalogue was written by Charles Hart, one of the first historians of American portraiture. He served on the Pennsylvania Academy's committee for exhibitions throughout the 1880s and 1890s and was probably the driving force behind the organization of portrait exhibitions during these years.

32 *Catalogue of a Collection of Portraits of the Colonial Period Exhibited by the Philobiblon Club*, exhib. cat. (Philadelphia: Pennsylvania Academy of the Fine Arts, 1893). The prints were lent from the collection of Clarence S. Bement.

33 Barbara Weinberg, "Thomas B. Clarke: Foremost Patron of American Art from 1872 to 1899," *American Art Journal* 8 (May 1976), pp. 52-83.

34 *Early American Portraits collected by Mr. Thomas B. Clarke* (New York: American Art Association, 1919), unpaginated.

35 *Portraits by Early American Artists of the Seventeenth, Eighteenth, and Nineteenth Centuries Collected by Thomas B. Clarke*, exhib. brochure (Philadelphia: Philadelphia Museum of Art, 1928). For a further description of the collection, see Cuthbert Lee, "The Thomas B. Clarke Collection of Early American Portraits," *American Magazine of Art* 19 (June 1928), pp. 292-305.

36 Lewis began making gifts from his collection a decade earlier, but the bulk of the collection was given to the Academy by his widow in 1933, with the stipulation that it be identified as the John Frederick Lewis Memorial Collection.

37 Mantle Fielding, *Exhibition of American Portraits, Collection of John Frederick Lewis*, exhib. cat. (Philadelphia: Pennsylvania Academy of the Fine Arts, 1934), p. 109.

38 Sawitsky's annotated copy of the Lewis collection catalogue is in the archives of the Pennsylvania Academy. Sawitsky was an advisory curator to the New-York Historical Society and the author of the *Catalogue Descriptive and Critical of the Paintings and Miniatures in the Historical Society of Pennsylvania* (Philadelphia: Historical Society of Pennsylvania, 1942).

39 John F. Lewis to Clement B. Newbold, March 21, 1916, John F. Lewis papers, Pennsylvania Academy Archives.

40 The commercial promotion of American folk art began in New York with the establishment of Edith Halpert's Downtown Gallery in 1926; see Diane Tepfer, "Edith Gregor Halpert and the Downtown Gallery: 1926-1940. A Study in Art Patronage," Ph.D. diss., University of Michigan, 1989. During this same period, scholars began to examine plain painting as a distinct aesthetic category within American art history; see Nina Fletcher Little, *Little by Little* (New York: E. P. Dutton, 1984), pp. 112-169.

41 Quoted in Susan Foister et al., *National Portrait Gallery Collection* (London: National Portrait Gallery, 1988), p. 112.

42 Philadelphia *Daily News*, Nov. 18, 1905. This review and others in the Pennsylvania Academy archives have been microfilmed (roll no. 54) by the Archives of American Art, Smithsonian Institution. A catalogue of the exhibition is in the Pennsylvania Academy Archives.

43 New York *Art Bulletin* (Dec. 2, 1905). Microfilm (roll no. 54), Archives of American Art.

44 Philadelphia *Public Ledger*, June 27, 1926.

45 *National Portrait Gallery, Smithsonian Institution, Permanent Collection, Illustrated Checklist* (Washington, D. C.: Smithsonian Institution Press, 1982), p. 6.

46 For example, lectures given by Ellen G. Miles, "Hidden Content Revealed: the Literary Source for Charles Willson Peale's Double Portrait of Benjamin and Eleanor Ridgely Laming," and Paul Staiti, "Accounting for Copley: The Portrait of John Hancock," at the Peale symposium "New Perspectives on America's Old Masters," April 13, 1991, organized by the National Portrait Gallery.

47 Elizabeth Johns, ed., *Seeing Women: Students Select from the Susan and Herbert Adler Collection of American Drawings and Watercolors*, exhib. cat. (Philadelphia: University of Pennsylvania, Arthur Ross Gallery, 1991).

Catalogue

The portraits in this catalogue are arranged by date of execution. Dimensions are given in inches and in centimeters; height precedes width.

Gilbert Stuart's image of George Washington (1732-1799) is arguably the best-known portrait in the history of American art. Painted from life in Stuart's Germantown studio in Philadelphia, the original version was commissioned by Martha Washington. Along with a portrait of her done at the same time, this work was meant to hang in the couple's home, Mount Vernon, in Virginia. Stuart kept the two unfinished portraits, however, and painted replicas on request. Over sixty are known to have been made of Washington. Stuart called this portrait his "hundred dollar bill" because that was the price he charged for producing a replica. The replica owned by the Pennsylvania Academy of the Fine Arts was made for a wealthy Philadelphia merchant, Paul Beck, Jr. The popularity of Stuart's image was due in great measure to the official recognition given to this portrait in 1826 when the House of Representatives stated that it believed Stuart's portrait to be the most faithful likeness of Washington.

After the artist's death, the unfinished portraits of both George and Martha Washington were purchased by the Boston Athenaeum, in 1831; and, since then, this portrait of Washington has been known as the Athenaeum head. (Today both paintings are owned jointly by the Museum of Fine Arts, Boston, and the National Portrait Gallery, Washington, D. C.). An engraving of the Athenaeum head appears on the one dollar bill.

References:

Mantle Fielding, *Gilbert Stuart's Portraits of George Washington*, Philadelphia: privately printed, 1923, pp. 99-112.

Egon Verheyen, "'The Most exact representation of the Original': Remarks on Portraits of George Washington by Gilbert Stuart and Rembrandt Peale," in *Retaining the Original, Multiple Originals, Copies, and Reproductions* (Center for Advanced Study in the Visual Arts, Symposium Papers, 7), Washington, D. C.: National Gallery of Art, 1989, pp. 127-139.

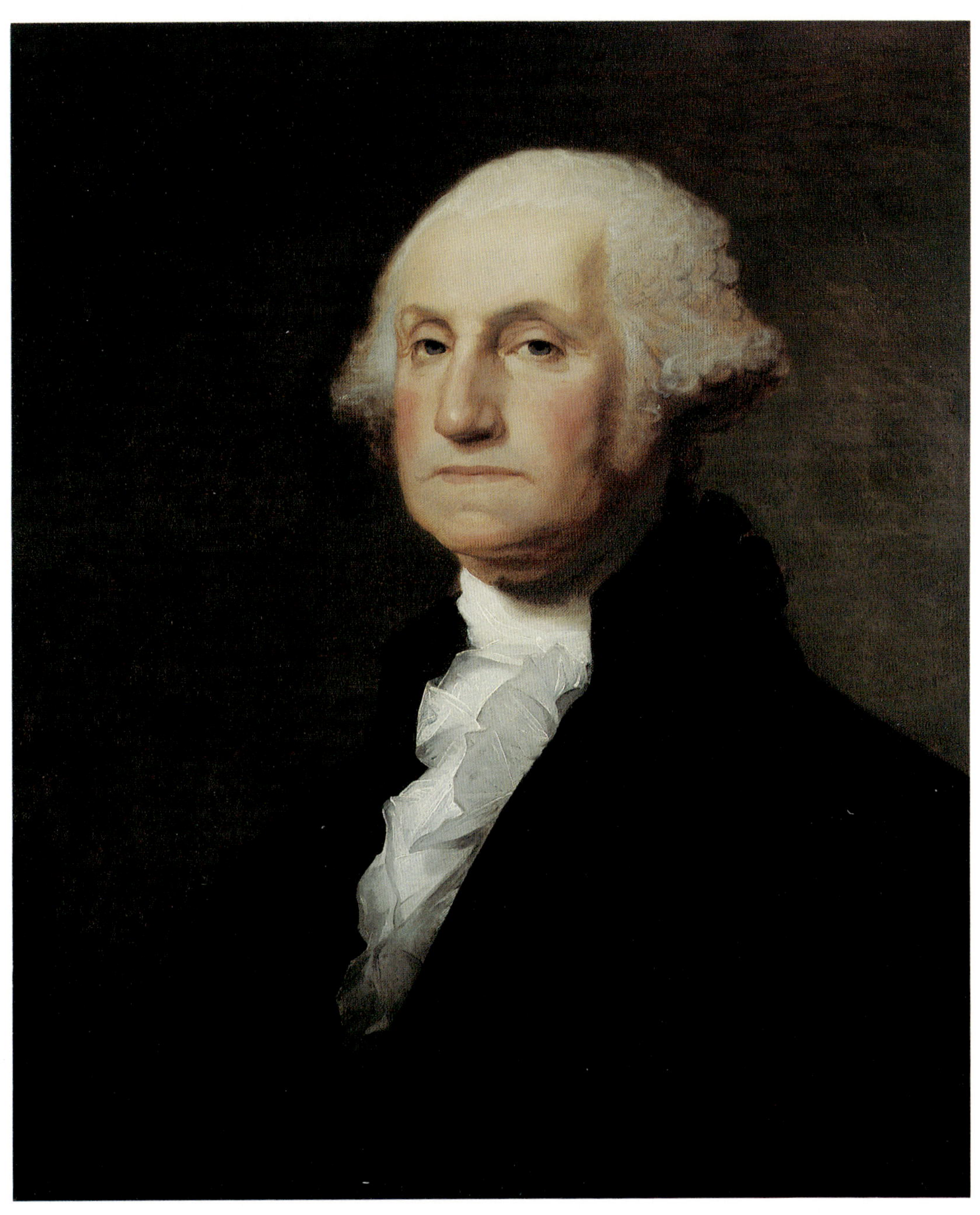

1
George Washington, after 1796
Oil on canvas
29 1/2 × 24 1/2 in. (74.9 × 62.2 cm)
Bequest of Paul Beck, Jr. 1845.3.2

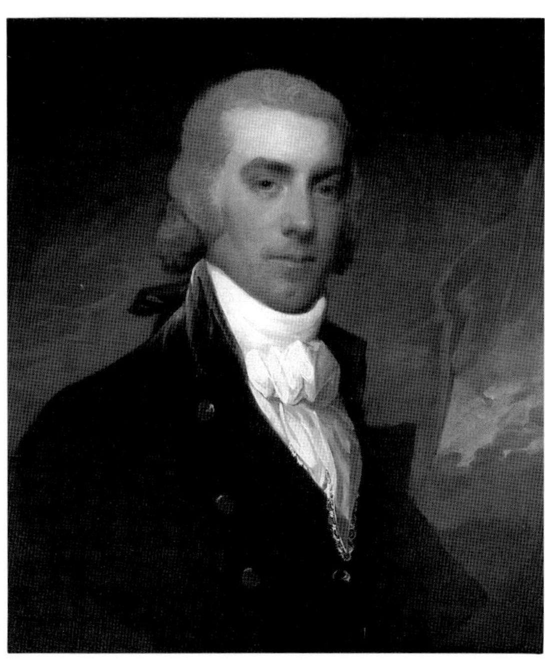

2
George Plumstead, 1800
Oil on canvas
29 1/4 × 24 1/4 in. (74.3 × 61.6 cm)
Bequest of Helen Ross Scheetz, 1891.12.1

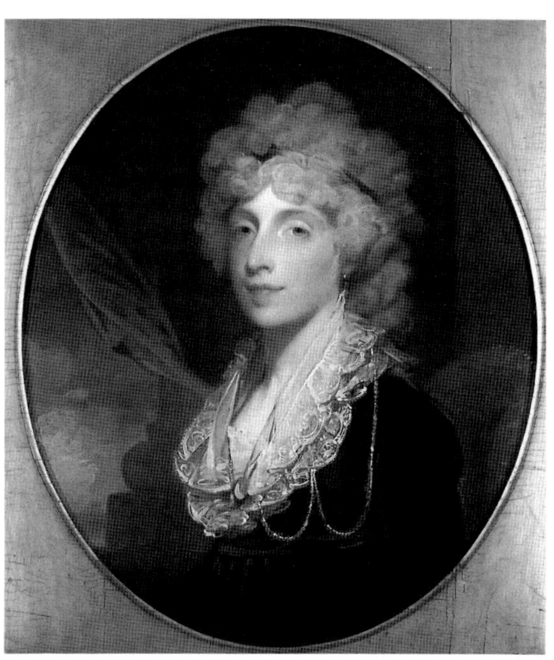

3
Mrs. George Plumstead, 1800
Oil on canvas
29 3/4 × 24 3/16 in. (74.6 × 61.4 cm)
Bequest of Helen Ross Scheetz, 1891.12.2

George Plumstead (1765-1805) was a Philadelphia merchant and a descendant of a prominent Quaker family. During the eighteenth century, both his father and grandfather had built the family's fortune and served as mayors of Philadelphia. In 1795, George married Anna Helena Amelia Ross (1776-1846). A few years later, he bought land on the Schuylkill River and built a large neoclassical house called Chamounix, finished in 1802. He and his wife also maintained a town house in Philadelphia, on Front Street below Pine. They belonged to Saint Peter's Episcopal Church, which counted George Washington among its socially prominent members. More extravagant in lifestyle and less successful in business than his forebears, George Plumstead died at the age of forty after accumulating an enormous debt. His wife, forced to sell the family property to support herself and their four children, managed to keep these portraits from the auction block. Later in the century, they passed to an heir who bequeathed them to the Pennsylvania Academy of the Fine Arts.

The Plumsteads were typical of the elite clientele that Gilbert Stuart sought as patrons. Wealthy and well connected, they were interested in having their likenesses painted by the most fashionable artist. Before he moved to Philadelphia in 1793, the American-born Stuart had spent almost two decades in England and Ireland, practicing the latest portrait styles. His freely painted surfaces, emphasis on the texture of lace and fancy powdered hairstyles, and background accoutrements, such as red curtains and classical columns, are adapted from the grand-manner portraits of Thomas Gainsborough and Sir Joshua Reynolds. Even after Stuart moved to Boston in 1805, his new European style had a great effect on Philadelphia portraiture, especially on the work of Thomas Sully (see cat. nos. 12, 16, and 29) and John Neagle (see cat. nos. 21 and 26).

References:

Gregory B. Keen, "The Descendants of Jöran Kyn, the Founder of Upland," *Pennsylvania Magazine* 6 (1882), pp. 106-110.

Eleanor Pearson DeLorme, "Gilbert Stuart, Portrait of an Artist," *Winterthur Portfolio* 14 (Winter 1979), pp. 339-360.

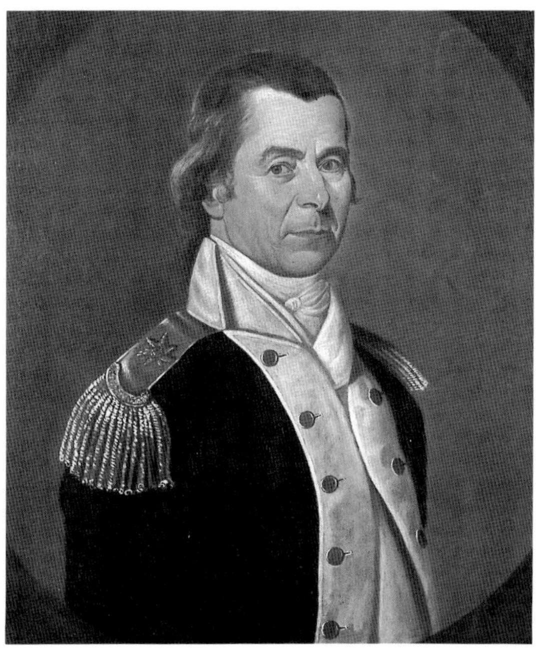

4
Colonel Constant Storrs, 1802
Oil on canvas
29 7/8 × 24 11/16 in. (75.9 × 62.7 cm)
Gift of John Frederick Lewis, 1923.8.16

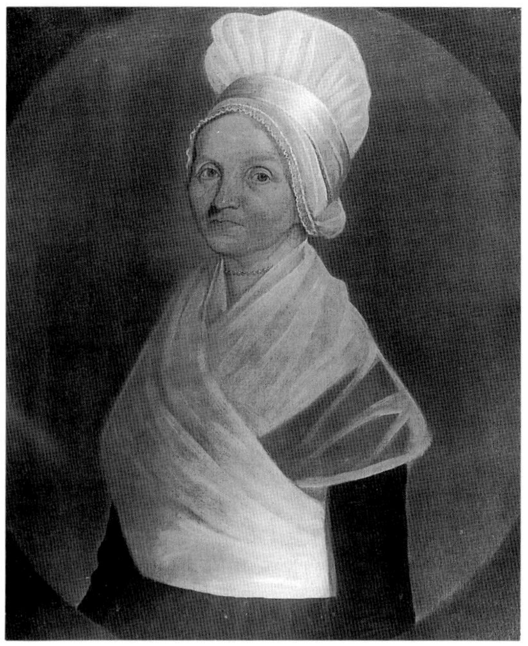

5
Mrs. Constant Storrs, probably 1802
Oil on canvas
29 7/8 × 24 11/16 in. (75.9 × 62.7 cm)
Gift of John Frederick Lewis, 1923.8.17

Constant and Lucinda Storrs were married in 1780 and had eight children over the course of the next twelve years. They lived in Lebanon, New Hampshire, where Colonel Storrs (1752-1828) was a prosperous farmer. According to a family genealogy, "he was noted for great firmness and decision of character: a man of dignified bearing, and of varied and extensive information, which he was ever ready to impart." His wife, Lucinda Howe Storrs (1758-1839), was descended from a prominent colonial family that had helped to settle Massachusetts and Connecticut. Orphaned at the age of nine, Lucinda soon developed a very religious frame of mind. She was an ardent reader of religious tracts and for many years kept a diary about her religious life (Connecticut Historical Society, Hartford). The diary is filled with poignant references to the deaths of her children, only one of whom survived her. Writing about herself and her husband, Lucinda Storrs lamented that "on a large farm, which subjected us to a great household of domestics, and engrossed so much of our time. . .we did not attend to the concerns of our souls so much as we ought to have done." A motto inscribed in the diary seems to sum up her approach to life: "Be moderate in prosperity and patient in adversity."

William Jennys's portraits of Colonel and Mrs. Storrs, executed in 1802, capture traits suggested by the written records of their lives. Colonel Storrs wears his revolutionary-war uniform as an indication of pride in the military days of his youth; his firmness is conveyed by the seriousness of his expression and stiff, upright pose. His wife's humility and piety are suggested by the simplicity of her costume and her rather grim, downturned mouth. Although Jennys was an itinerant painter with no academic training in portraiture, he clearly was capable of capturing a convincing likeness.

References:

Charles Storrs, *The Storrs Family Genealogical and Other Memorabilia*, New York: privately printed, 1886, pp. 312-315.

William Lamson Warren, "The Jennys Portraits," *Connecticut Historical Society Bulletin* 20 (Oct. 1955), pp. 112-115, and 21 (April 1956), pp. 61-62.

1755–1828

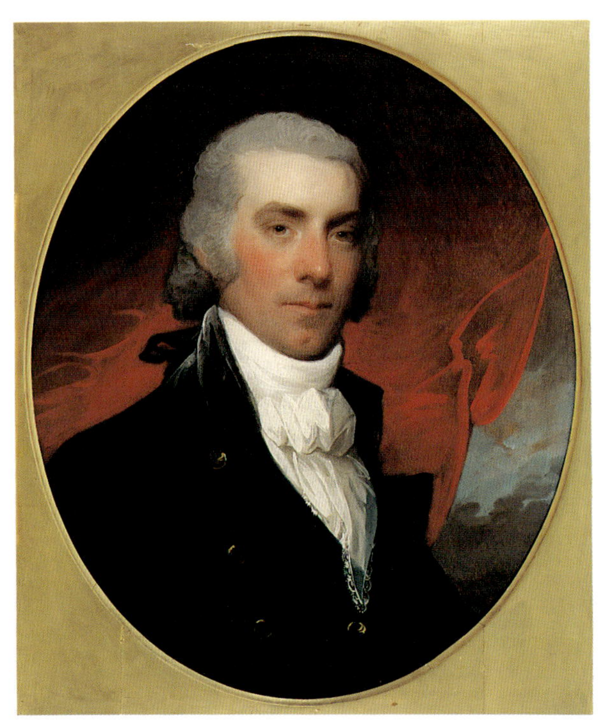

2
George Plumstead, 1800

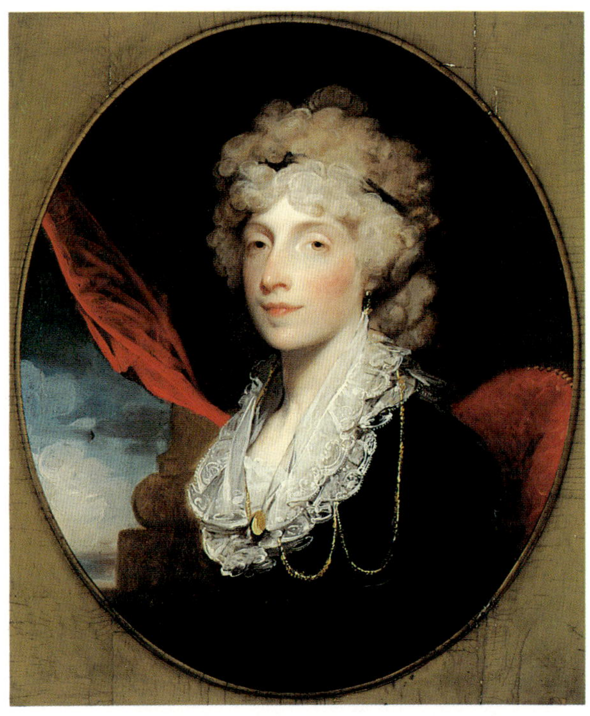

3
Mrs. George Plumstead, 1800

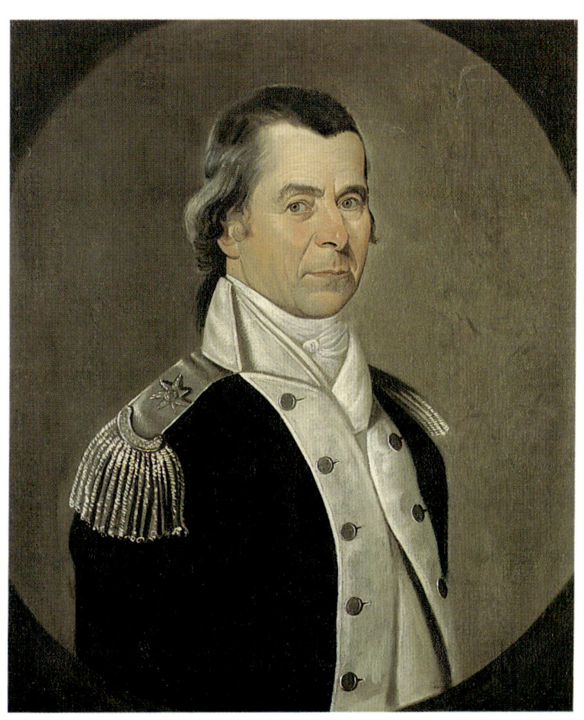

4
Colonel Constant Storrs, 1802

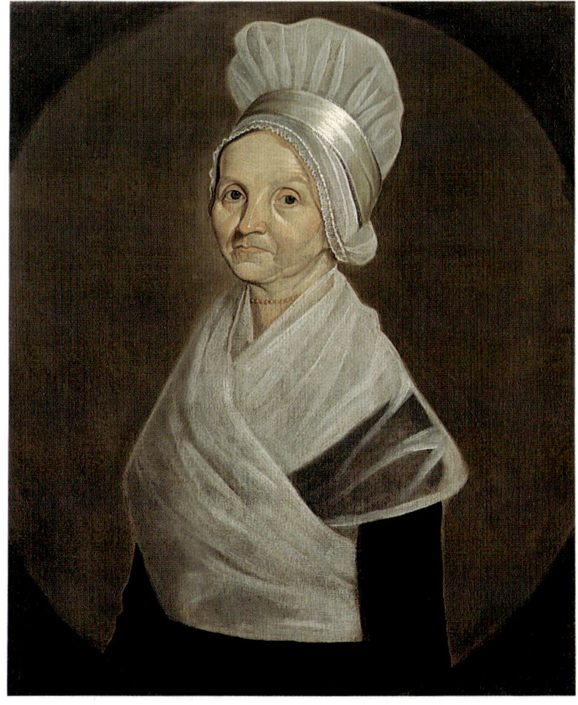

5
Mrs. Constant Storrs, probably 1802

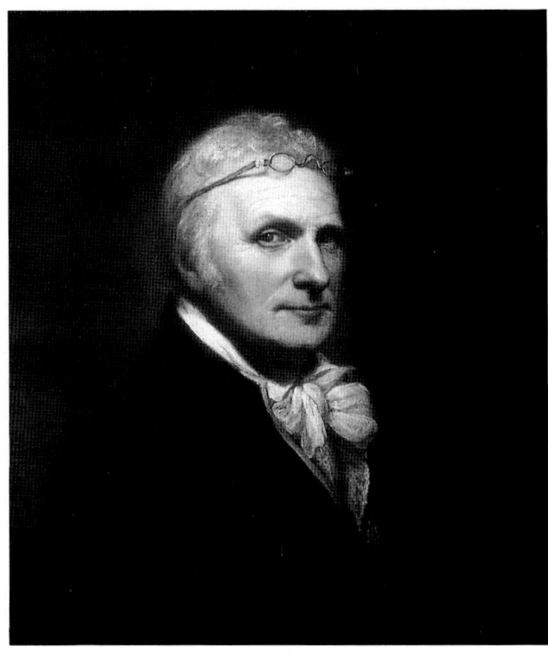

6
Self-Portrait with Spectacles, ca. 1804
Oil on canvas, mounted on wood
26 3/16 × 22 5/16 in. (66.5 × 56.7 cm)
Henry D. Gilpin Fund, 1939.18

Charles Willson Peale was one of the most prolific American portraitists of the late eighteenth and early nineteenth centuries. He painted revolutionary-war heroes and statesmen, wealthy landowners and their families, scientists, and intellectuals. Over the course of his long career, he also produced at least seventeen self-portraits, many of which were given to his children as wedding presents. *Self-Portrait with Spectacles* was painted when the artist was over sixty years old. At that time, he was much involved in the founding of the Pennsylvania Academy of the Fine Arts and the running of his own museum of art and natural history. Peale's museum, located in Independence Hall, displayed portraits of notable Americans above cases filled with stuffed birds and animals (see fig. 1). Intended to serve as exemplars of great deeds, such portraits were installed with the natural history specimens as symbols of evolutionary progress.

The inclusion of eyeglasses in this self-portrait is another example of Peale's use of symbolism. A realist in his approach to painting, he no doubt included his glasses because he used them; but they can also be seen as a metaphor for artistic and scientific vision. They appear as a conspicuous motif not only in Peale's self-portraits but also in his paintings of other family members, such as the 1822 portrait of his artist brother, James (Detroit Institute of Arts; see also cat. no. 7). Charles Willson Peale's son Rembrandt painted two self-portraits with glasses, one dated 1828 (Detroit Institute of Arts) and another about 1845 (cat. no. 30); and there are two pairs of spectacles in his portrait of his brother, *Rubens Peale with a Geranium* (1801, National Gallery of Art, Washington, D. C.). Once established as a motif by the Peale family, the depiction of eyeglasses in artists' portraits became common in the nineteenth century. There are several examples in the collection of the Pennsylvania Academy, including self-portraits by Jacob Eichholtz, dated 1834; George P. A. Healy, dated 1881; and Robert Vonnoh, dated 1901. (For works by these artists in this catalogue, see cat. nos. 23, 31, and 40, respectively.)

References:

Charles Coleman Sellers, *Portraits and Miniatures by Charles Willson Peale*, Philadelphia: American Philosophical Society, 1952, no. 631.

Ann C. Van Devanter et al., *American Self-Portraits*, 1670-1973, exhib. cat., New York: E. P. Dutton for International Exhibitions Foundation, 1974, no. 14.

1749–1831

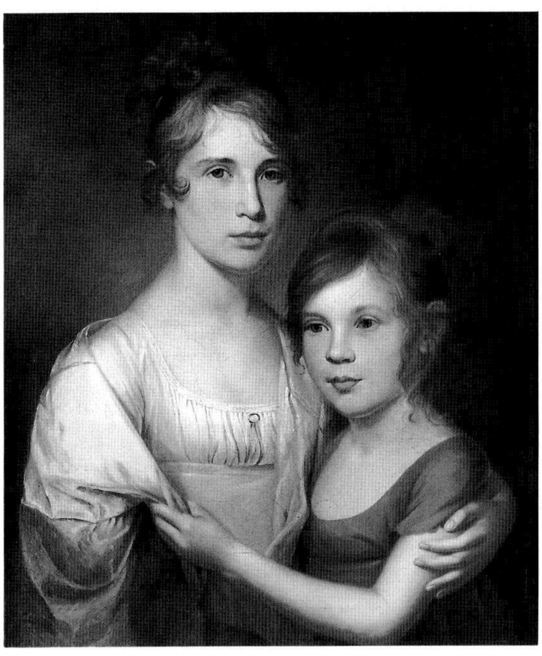

7
Anna and Margaretta Peale, ca. 1805
Oil on canvas
29 × 24 in. (73.7 × 61 cm)
Pennsylvania Academy purchase, 1902.5

These two young girls were the daughters of James Peale, Philadelphia's leading miniature painter at the beginning of the nineteenth century. Trained to paint portraits by his brother Charles Willson Peale (see cat. no. 6), James went on to specialize in miniatures and still lifes. His daughters, in turn, became artists and practiced the same kinds of painting in which he excelled. In this portrait, the encircling gesture of their arms suggests the close relationship for which the Peale family is noted.

Anna (1791-1878), on the left, was a miniature painter and one of the first professional women artists in the United States. She showed her work frequently in the annual exhibitions at the Pennsylvania Academy of the Fine Arts between 1811 and 1842 and was elected an academician in 1824. Among the sitters for her miniatures were two United States presidents (James Monroe and Andrew Jackson), a number of diplomats, and many clients from Boston to Richmond. Most of her career, however, was spent in Philadelphia and Baltimore, where she maintained a studio in the family's second museum. (The original museum, as noted in the previous entry, was in Philadelphia.) Anna's younger sister Margaretta Angelica (1795-1882) practiced still-life painting for the most part and was not as active professionally. Between 1828 and 1837, she showed several still lifes and one portrait in the annual exhibitions of the Pennsylvania Academy. Another sister, Sarah Miriam, also became a portrait painter (see cat. no. 18).

References:

The Peale Family, exhib. cat., Detroit: Detroit Institute of Arts, 1967, no. 74.

Robert Devlin Schwarz, *A Gallery Collects Peales*, exhib. cat., Philadelphia: Frank S. Schwarz and Son, 1987, pp. 60-63.

1741–1827

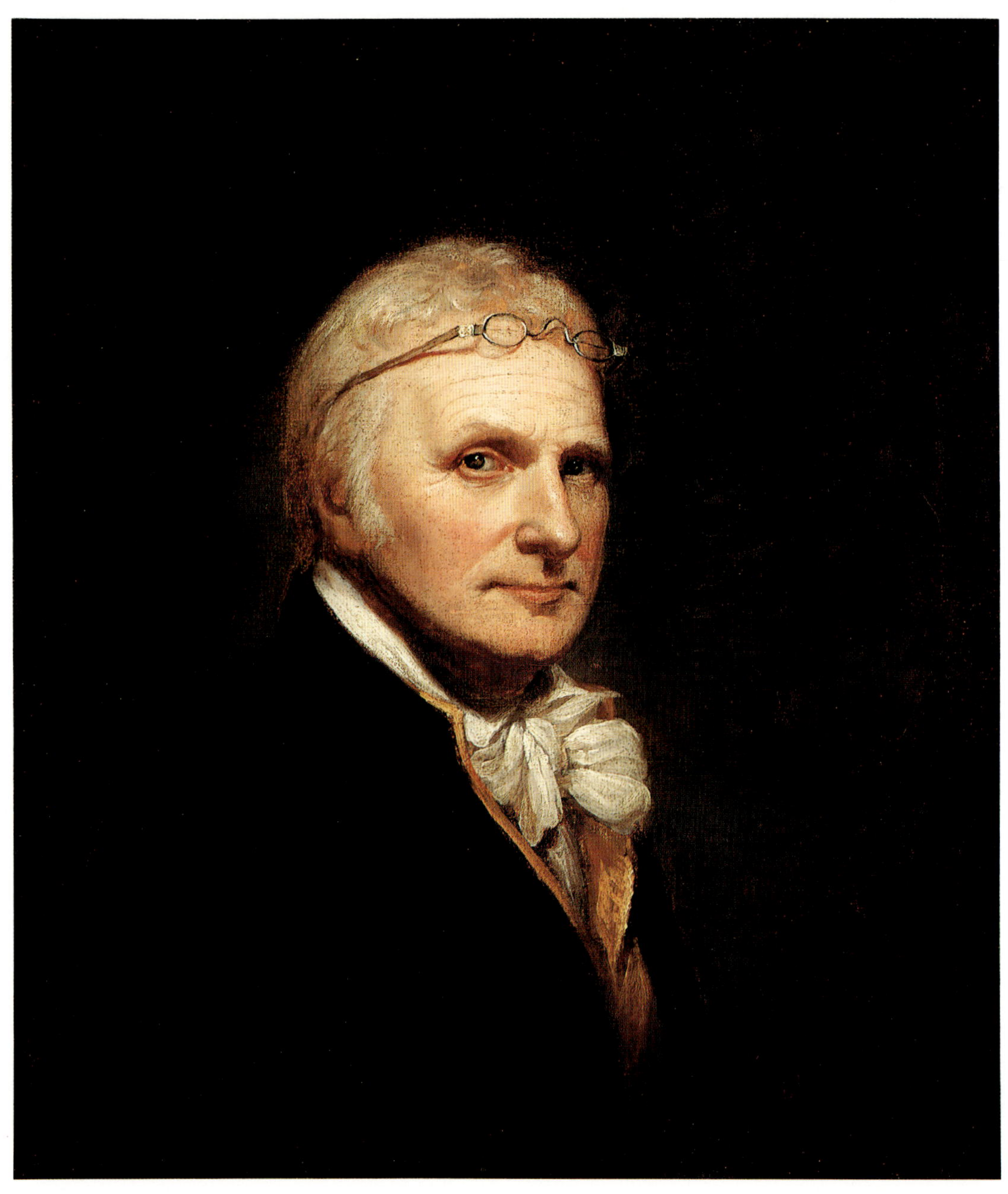

6

Self-Portrait with Spectacles, ca. 1804

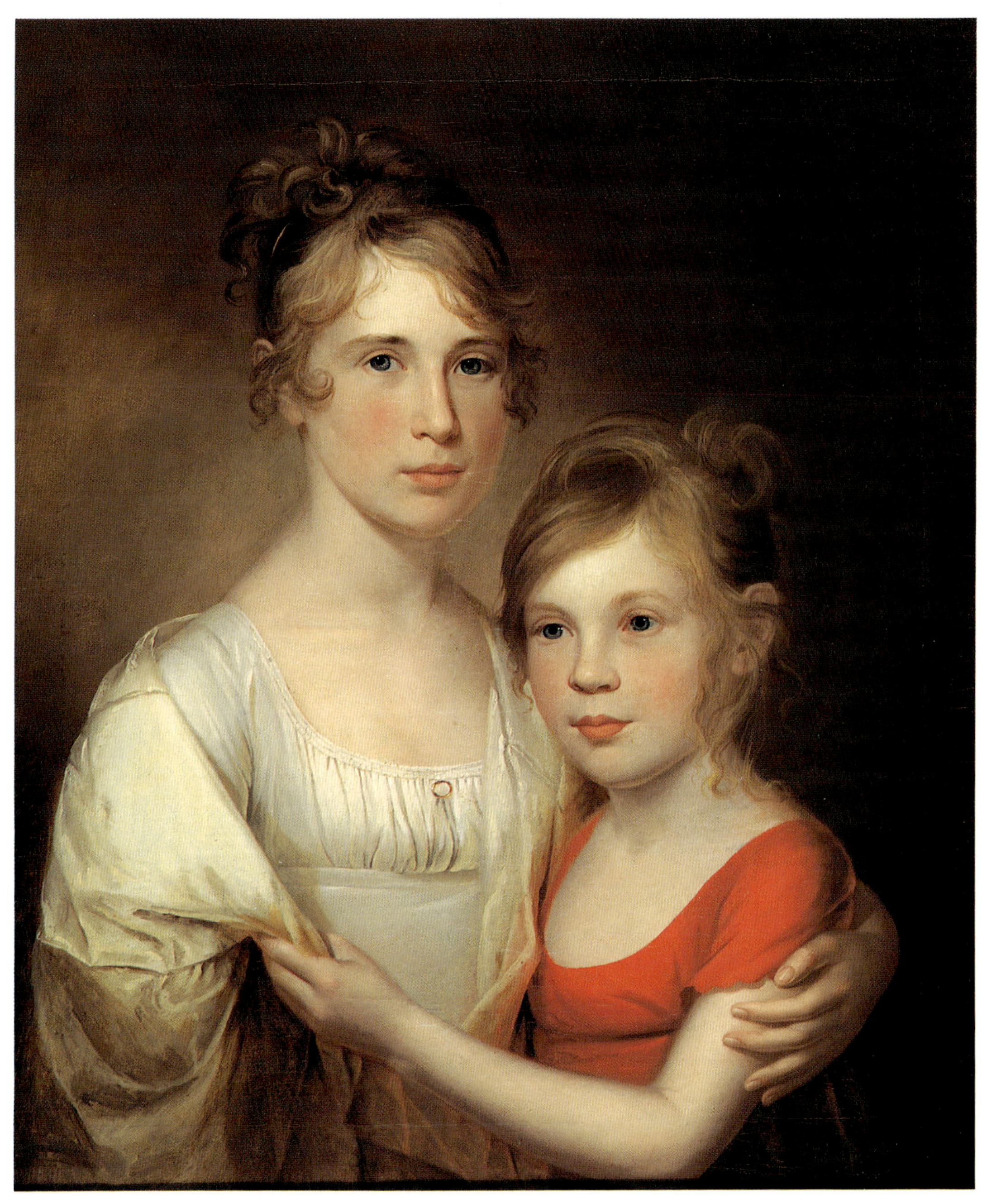

7
Anna and Margaretta Peale, ca. 1805

1738–1820

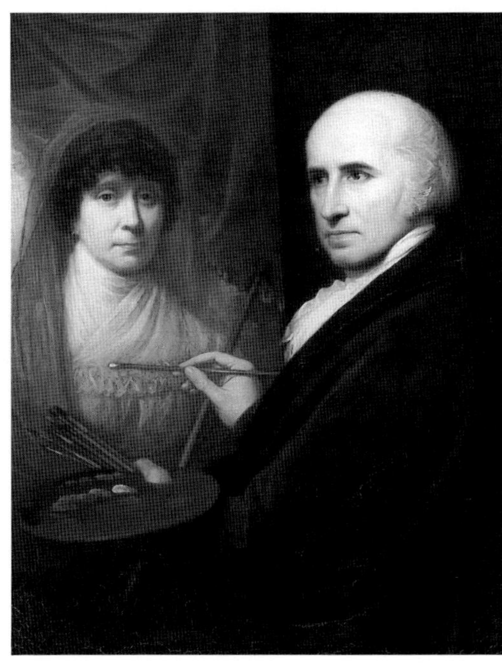

8
Self-Portrait, 1806
Oil on canvas
36⅛ in. (91.8 × 71.4 cm)
Gift of Mr. and Mrs. Henry R. Hallowell, 1964.11

•

Benjamin West gave this self-portrait to the artist and inventor Robert Fulton (1765-1815) in 1806 as a token of their friendship and their common bond as Pennsylvania-born artists. At the time, West held the prestigious position of president of the Royal Academy in London. Although he had begun his artistic career as a portraitist, his reputation was based primarily on paintings of historical and literary subjects. While in London, Fulton assembled a collection of works by West and European artists, which he intended to give to the newly founded Pennsylvania Academy of the Fine Arts on his return to the United States. This portrait and other works from Fulton's collection were exhibited at the Pennsylvania Academy from 1808 until 1816 as models of academic art for American artists to study.

The portrait shows West in the act of painting a likeness of his wife, Elizabeth Shewell West (1741-1814). There are important precedents for this kind of self-portraiture not only in American art but also in sixteenth-century Netherlandish painting. Charles Willson Peale's *Self-Portrait with Angelica and a Portrait of Rachel* (ca. 1782-85, Museum of Fine Arts, Houston) shows a similar illusionistically painted portrait-within-a-portrait. Peale (see cat. no. 6), who had studied with West in London, was a founder of the Pennsylvania Academy and worked closely with Fulton in planning the installation of his collection there. Portraits by Peale and West, in turn, must have provided inspiration for other Pennsylvania painters, such as John Neagle (see cat. nos. 21 and 26) and James R. Lambdin (see cat. no. 37).

References:

Helmut von Erffa and Allen Staley, *The Paintings of Benjamin West*, New Haven: Yale University Press, 1986, no. 530.

Carrie Rebora, "Robert Fulton's Art Collection," *American Art Journal* 22 (Fall 1990), pp. 40-63.

David Steinberg, "Charles Willson Peale, The Portraitist as Divine," in *New Perspectives on Charles Willson Peale*, Lillian B. Miller and David C. Ward, eds., Pittsburgh: University of Pittsburgh Press, 1991, pp. 131-143.

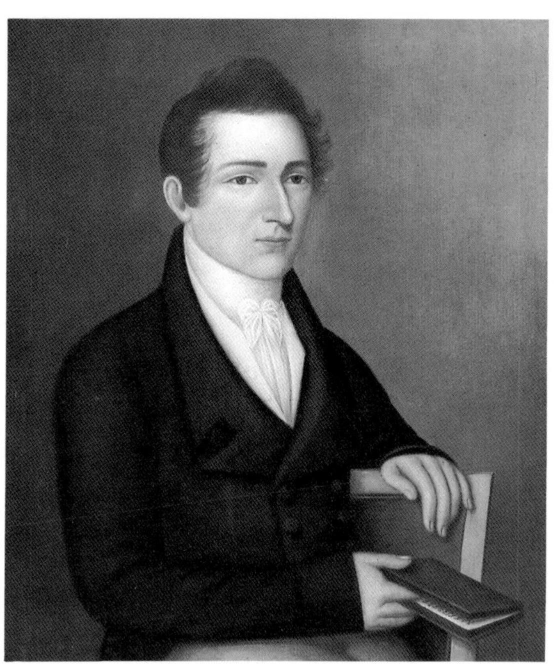

9
Unidentified Man, ca. 1810
Oil on canvas
26 1/8 × 22 1/16 in. (66.4 × 56 cm)
Gift of Mrs. Edgar L. Smith, 1980.5.2

•

Joshua Johnson is the first African-American artist to whom a substantial body of work has been attributed—all of it portraiture. Scholars believe that he was probably a slave brought to Baltimore from the West Indies by a privateer, the father of the portrait painter Charles Peale Polk (1767-1822), who was the nephew of Charles Willson Peale (see cat. no. 6). Johnson may have worked as a valet for the Peale family in Philadelphia and learned to paint there. By 1798, he had become a free man and was advertising his services as a portrait painter in Baltimore newspapers.

Although he was most likely self-taught, Johnson clearly understood the academic tradition practiced by Peale and others. The fashionable, upswept Napoleonic hairstyle of the sitter and the careful arrangement of his three-quarter pose can be found in any number of portraits produced by academically trained portraitists of the period. But Johnson's dependence on outline, simple modeling, and the use of bold, flat colors are characteristic of the American "plain style" that coexisted alongside the academic tradition in the early nineteenth century.

Reference:

Carolyn J. Weekly et al., *Joshua Johnson, Freeman and Early American Portrait Painter*, exhib. cat., Williamsburg: Abby Aldrich Rockefeller Folk Art Center, Colonial Williamsburg Foundation, 1987, p. 133.

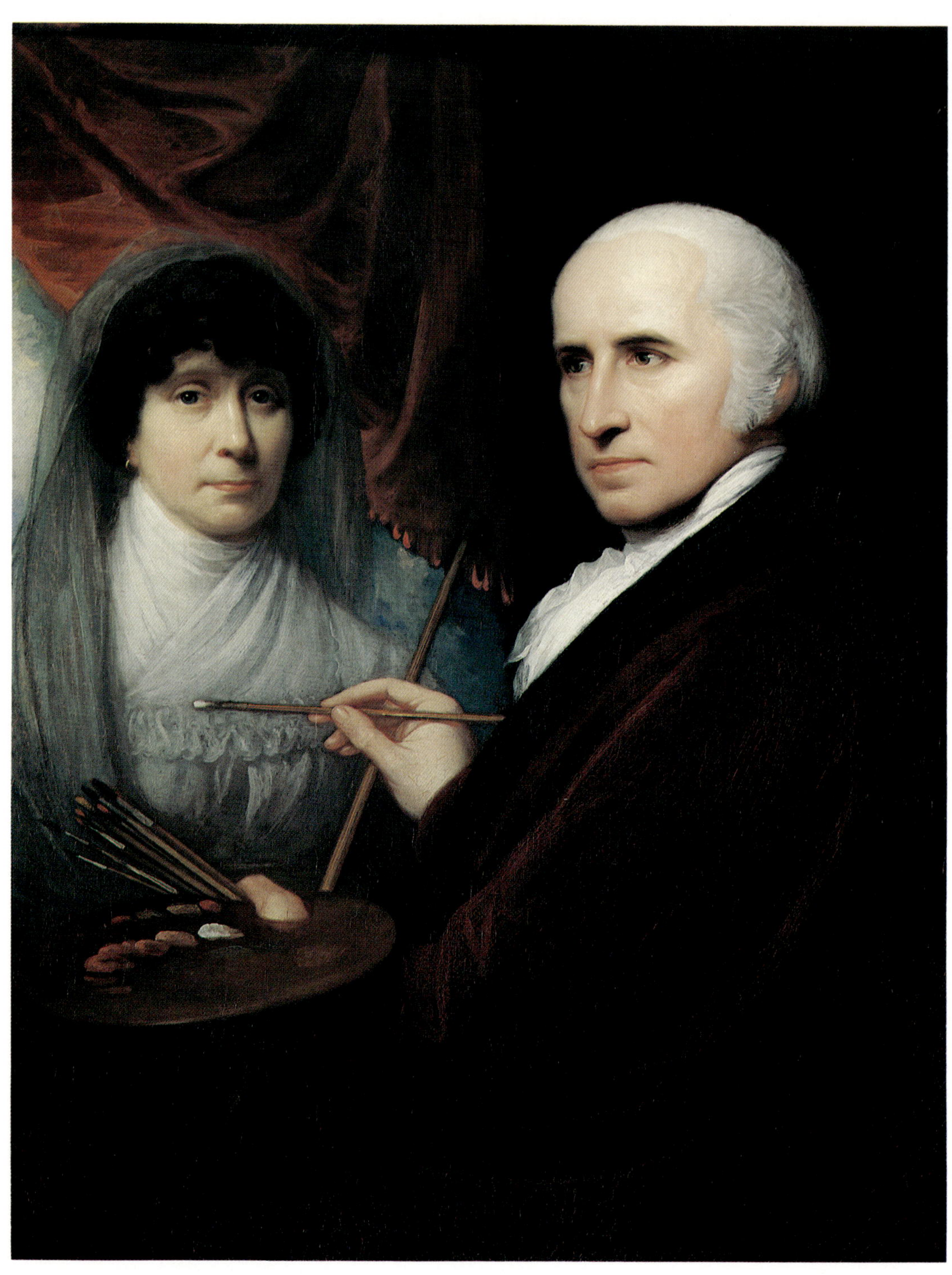

8
SELF-PORTRAIT, 1806

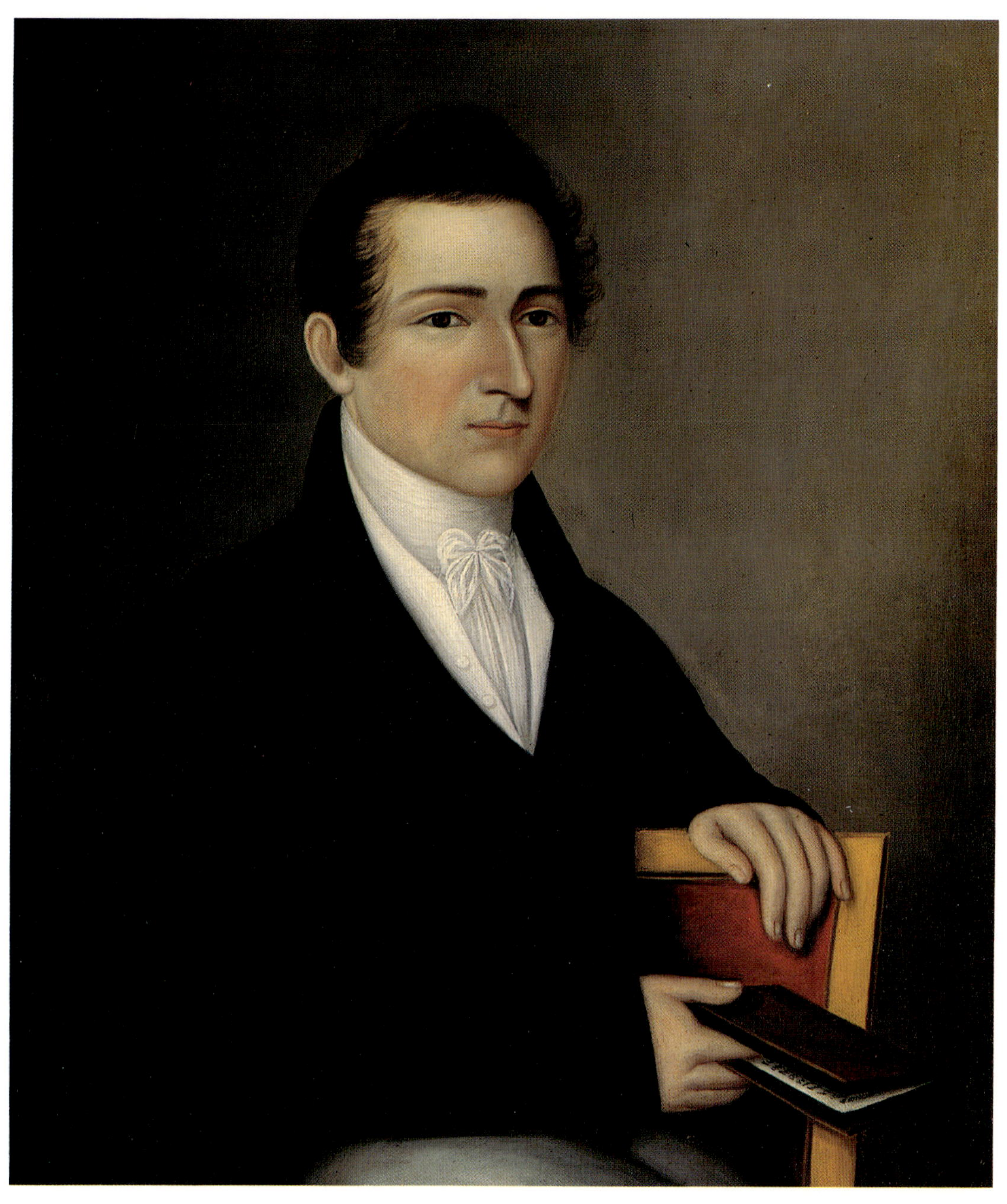

9
Unidentified Man, ca. 1810

1783–1833

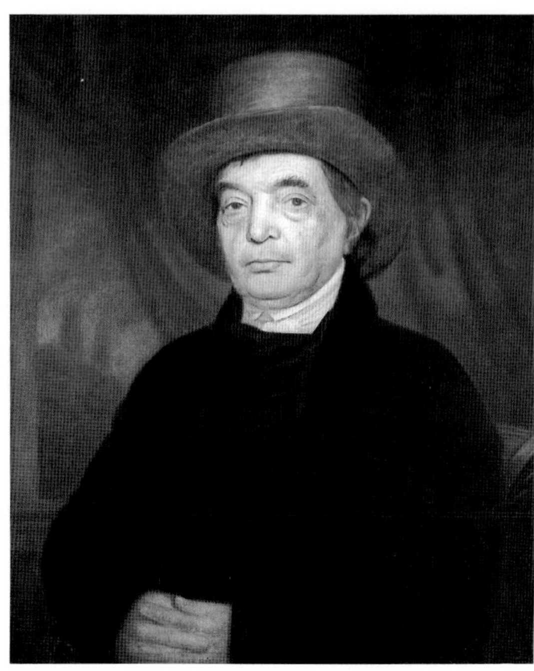

10

Philip Arcularius, ca. 1810
Oil on canvas
29 7/8 × 23 3/4 in. (75.9 × 60.3 cm)
Gift of John Frederick Lewis, Jr., 1952.3.1

John Paradise was a New Jersey-born artist, who received his early training from Denis A. Volozon, a French neo-classical artist active in Philadelphia between 1799 and 1819. In 1810, Paradise moved to New York, where he settled for the rest of his career. This work depicts a successful New York tanner and currier, Philip Arcularius (ca. 1750-1824/25), who had been appointed superintendent of the city's almshouse in 1805. The tall beaver hat that he wears is a symbol of his pride in civic office. Such hats were often worn in his native Germany, where he had served as burgomaster of the town of Marburg; and they also appear in seventeenth-century Dutch portraits of city officials.

The high degree of realism in this portrait—the attention paid to the sitter's bushy eyebrows, the pouches under his eyes, and his double chin—also links this work to the Dutch portrait tradition. Dutch portraitists introduced realistically rendered images of the bourgeoisie to the history of art; and the popularity of this kind of portraiture spread to the American colonies, where it remained predominant until the beginning of the nineteenth century. Unlike Philadelphia portrait painters, such as Gilbert Stuart (see cat. nos. 1–3) and Thomas Sully (see cat. nos. 16 and 29), who tended to generalize and idealize the facial features of sitters, Paradise emphasized the individuality of his subjects. The portrait in the collection of the Pennsylvania Academy is a replica of one at the New-York Historical Society.

Reference:

Catalogue of American Portraits in the New-York Historical Society, New Haven: Yale University Press, 1974, vol. 1, p. 24, no. 52.

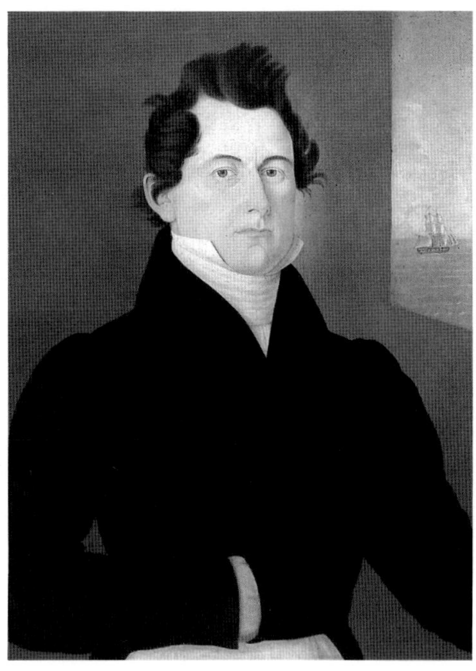

11
Unidentified Man, ca. 1810
Oil on canvas
30 7/16 × 22 1/8 in. (77.3 × 56.2 cm)
Gift of John Frederick Lewis, 1932.13.6

Background details were often used to identify the profession or social position of the subject of a portrait. The sitter here was most likely a sea captain or merchant, as indicated by the distant sailing ship seen through the window. This kind of pictorial convention, adopted from European art, was first introduced into colonial portraiture in the late seventeenth century; and by the nineteenth century, it had become a standard iconographic device for both self-taught and academically trained artists.

Judging from the fashionable Napoleonic pose, style of clothing, and upswept hairstyle worn by the sitter in this work, it was probably painted about 1810. The simplicity of the background, the linear handling of the sitter's facial features, and the omission of the hands, which are difficult to render, suggest that the painter was self-taught. Works in this "plain style" have often been described as folk art. Scholars have recently suggested, however, that this kind of American portraiture should be distinguished from true folk art. Because these plain portraits are so dependent on traditional aesthetic forms and concerned with the social or economic status of the sitter, they reinforce a sense of social hierarchy. Folk art, on the other hand, has generally turned its back on academic tradition. Created by a small group of craftsmen with common ethnic, religious, or geographic bonds, folk art is less elitist and is directed toward shared community interests rather than social or economic stratifications.

References:

Mantle Fielding, *Exhibition of American Portraits, Collection of John Frederick Lewis*, exhib. cat., Philadelphia: Pennsylvania Academy of the Fine Arts, 1934, no. 182.

John Michael Vlach, *Plain Painters: Making Sense of American Folk Art*, Washington, D. C.: Smithsonian Institution Press, 1988, pp. 1-86.

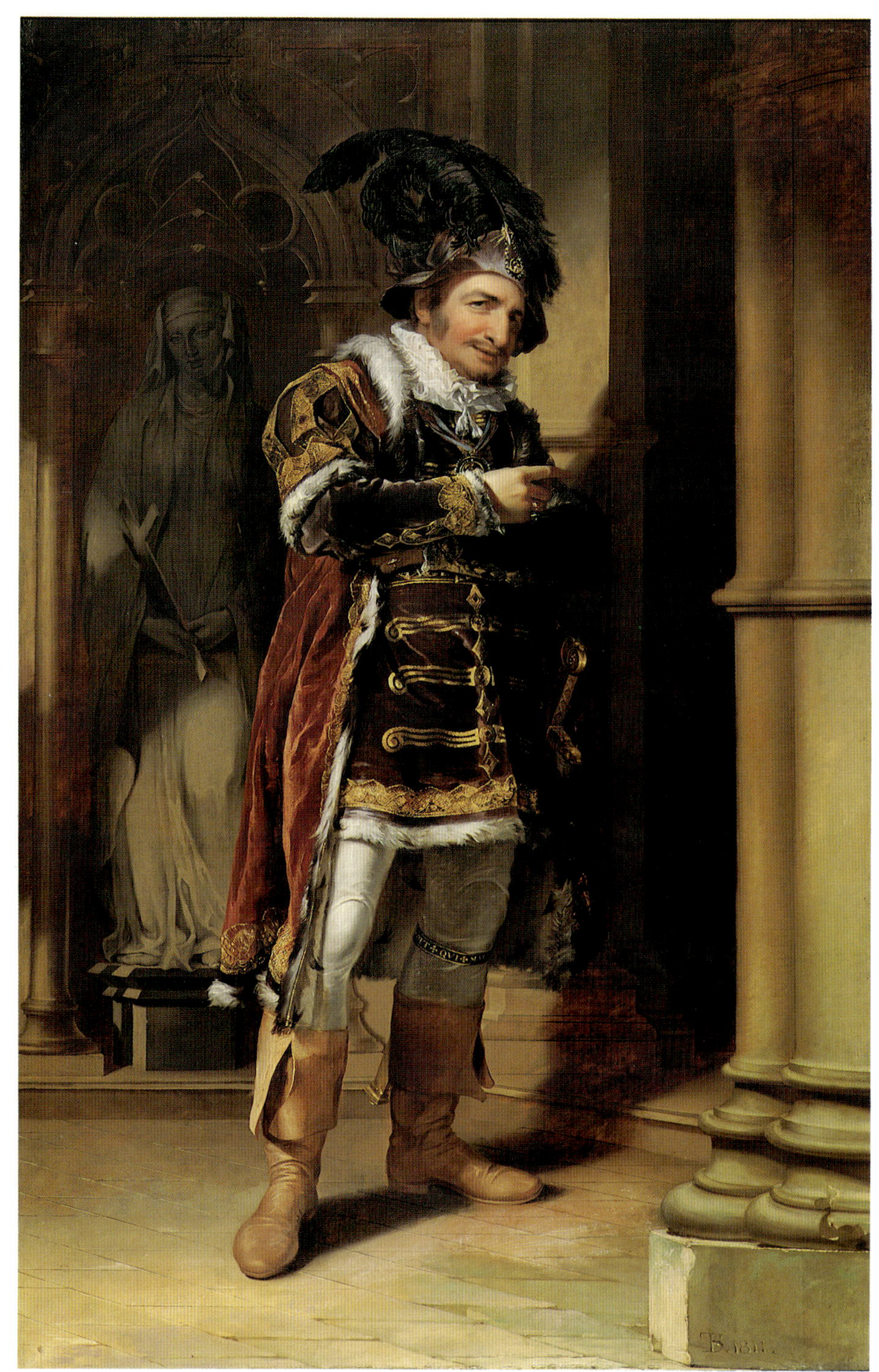

12
George Frederick Cooke as Richard III, 1811–12

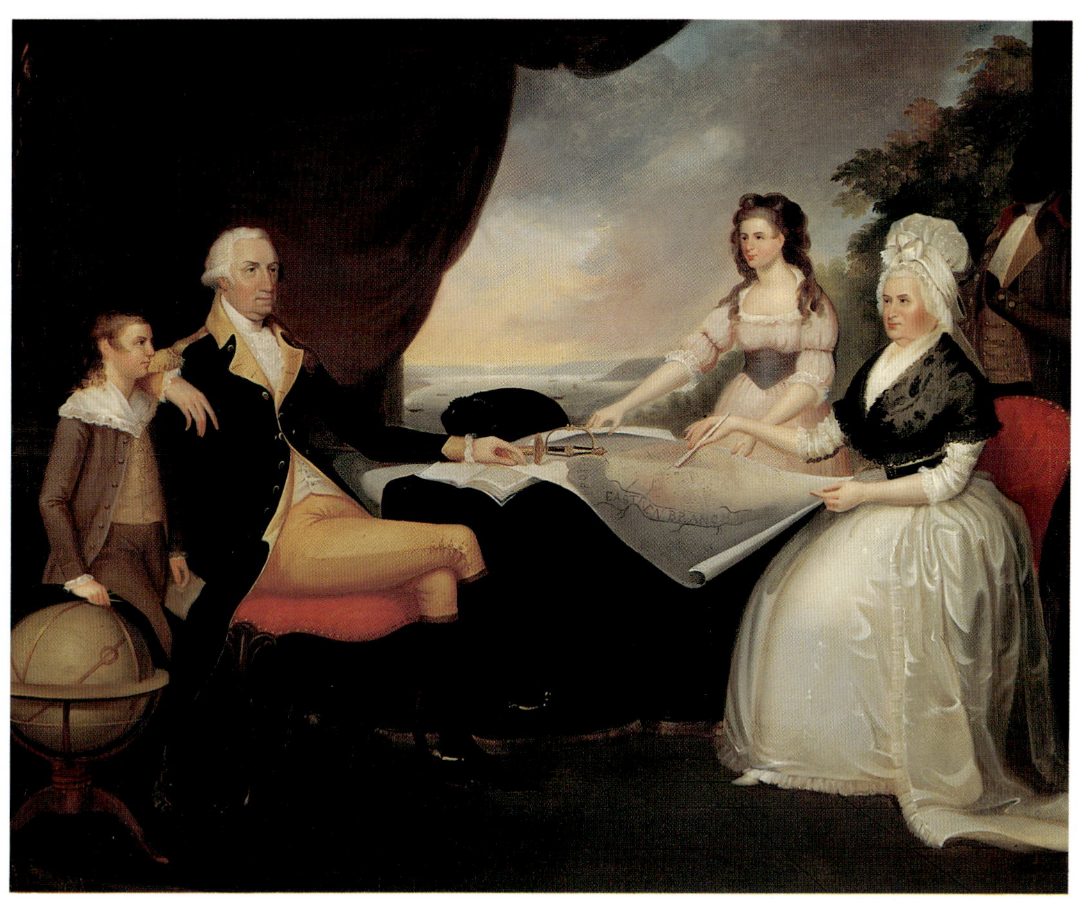

13

Washington Family at Mount Vernon, ca. 1815

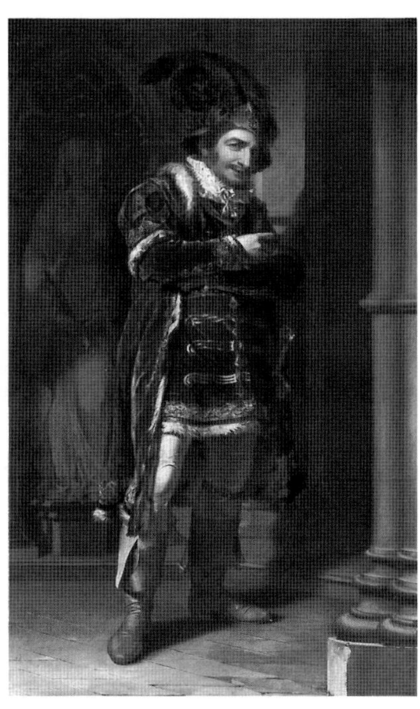

12
George Frederick Cooke as Richard III, 1811–12
Oil on canvas
94 7/8 × 60 1/2 in. (241 × 153.7 cm)
Gift of friends and admirers of the artist, 1812.1

Thomas Sully's portrait of the British actor George Frederick Cooke (1756-1812) firmly established the artist's reputation as the leading portrait painter in Philadelphia. The son of actors himself, Sully began his career as a miniature painter but turned to easel painting in 1805 in New York, where some of his earliest patrons were theater people. He then studied briefly with Gilbert Stuart in Boston (see cat. nos. 1-3) and in 1808 settled in Philadelphia. Shortly after returning from a trip to London, where he had studied with Benjamin West (see cat. no. 8) and Sir Thomas Lawrence, Sully received a commission from a group of theater enthusiasts to paint a portrait of Cooke for three hundred dollars. The patrons requested that Cooke pose in the title role of Shakespeare's *Richard III*, which he was then performing in Philadelphia.

Cooke, noted for his powerful soliloquies, is shown delivering four lines from Shakespeare's *Henry VI, Part III*, which he inserted for dramatic effect into the performances of *Richard III*:

> Why I can smile, and murther whiles I smile,
> And cry "Content" to that which grieves my heart,
> And wet my cheeks with artificial tears,
> And frame my face to all occasions.
> (Act 3, scene 2, lines 182-185)

When the actor died suddenly the following year, Sully's portrait was put on display at Philadelphia's Chestnut Street Theatre for a memorial service. The success of the Cooke portrait led Sully to paint several portraits of other popular theatrical figures, including Charles and Frances Anne (Fanny) Kemble (1833 and 1836, respectively, Pennsylvania Academy of the Fine Arts).

References:

Michael Quick, *American Portraits in the Grand Manner: 1720-1920*, exhib. cat., Los Angeles: Los Angeles County Museum of Art, 1981, pp. 128-129.

Christopher M. S. Johns, "Theater and Theory, Thomas Sully's 'George Frederick Cooke as Richard III,'" *Winterthur Portfolio* 18 (Spring 1983), pp. 28-38.

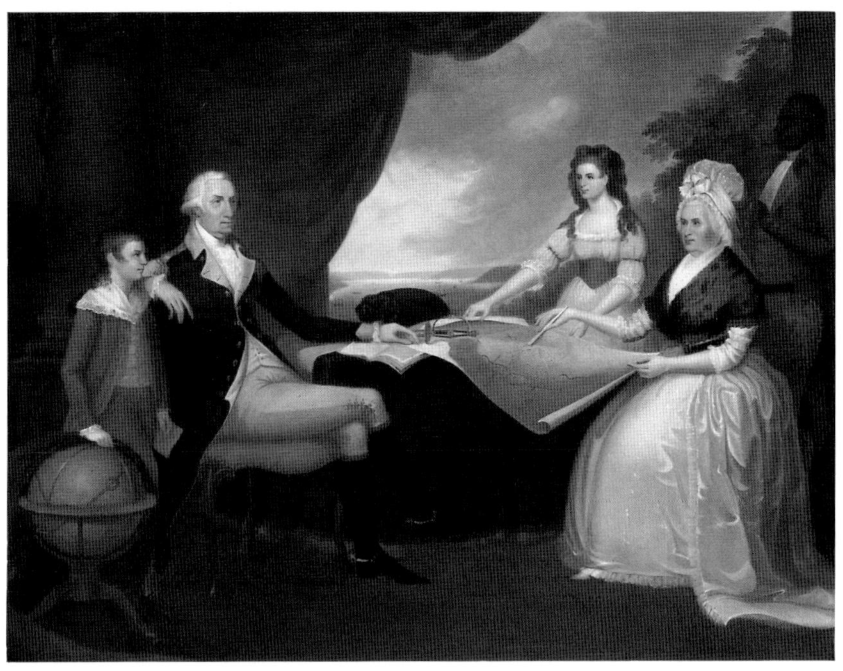

13
Washington Family at Mount Vernon, ca. 1815
(after Edward Savage, 1796)
Oil on canvas, 29 1/16 × 36 1/4 in. (73.8 × 92.1 cm)
Gift of Mrs. John Frederick Lewis (The John Frederick Lewis Memorial Collection), 1933.10.101

Paintings called conversation pieces, which showed the sitters grouped informally around a table or out-of-doors, were a popular form of portraiture in eighteenth-century England. This American conversation piece depicts George Washington at Mount Vernon, his home in Virginia, beside the Potomac River, which can be seen in the background. He is surrounded by his wife; her two grandchildren, Custis and Nellie; and one of the family slaves, Billy Lee. While notable portraits of the period by Charles Willson Peale and Gilbert Stuart emphasize Washington's role as a military leader or statesman (1779 and 1796, respectively, Pennsylvania Academy of the Fine Arts), this portrait conveys his interest in the plans for the nation's new capital, Washington, D. C. A map of the proposed city lies on the table before him. When Savage began work on Washington's portrait in 1789, Philadelphia was still the capital; but, by the time the portrait was completed in 1796, construction of the new seat of government was well underway.

Savage's image of Washington as both a family man and a city planner had great popular appeal during the early nineteenth century. Savage had the work engraved in 1798 as a moneymaking enterprise. John Wesley Jarvis (see cat. no. 19), then working as his apprentice, collaborated on its production. Other artists also painted copies of Savage's original (now in the National Gallery of Art, Washington, D. C.). This unattributed copy was probably made in Philadelphia about 1815; it is one of two small replicas in the collection of the Pennsylvania Academy of the Fine Arts. In the mid-nineteenth century, this well-known image was even copied on a window shade.

References:

Mantle Fielding, "Edward Savage's Portraits of George Washington," *Pennsylvania Magazine of History and Biography* 48, no. 3 (1924), pp. 195-196.

Harold E. Dickson, *John Wesley Jarvis, American Painter, 1780-1840*, New York: New-York Historical Society, 1949, pp. 35-57.

Wendy C. Wick, *George Washington, An American Icon*, exhib. cat., Washington, D. C.: National Portrait Gallery, 1982, pp. 40-44, no. 55.

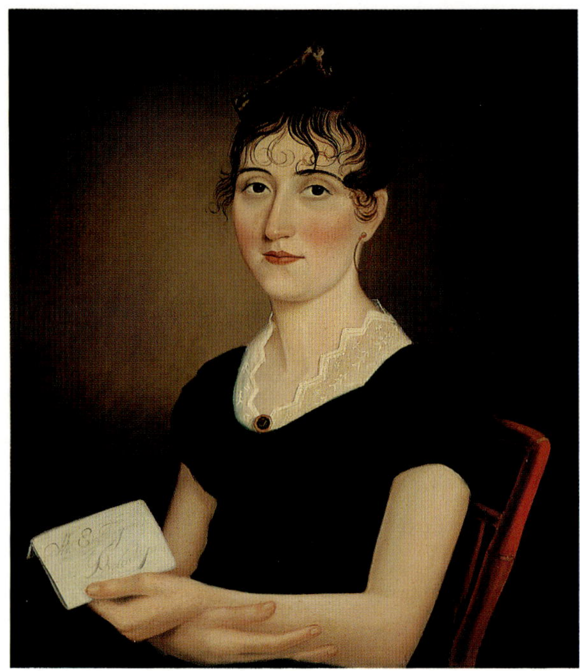

14
Unidentified Woman, ca. 1815
Oil on canvas,
26 × 22 15/16 in. (66 × 58.3 cm)
Gift of John Frederick Lewis, 1932.13.8

There are several elements in this unidentified portrait that provide information about its date and origin. The sitter holds a letter that bears a partially obscured inscription—"M. E. Tay[?]/Philadelphia"—most likely her name and place of residence. The style of her fashionable Empire dress and distinctive hairdo with loose curls and tortoiseshell comb date the work to the decade between 1810 and 1820. Although once attributed to Bass Otis (1784-1861), a Philadelphia portrait painter active during this period, this work differs considerably from his academic paintings. For example, Otis's portrait (ca. 1815, Pennsylvania Academy of the Fine Arts) of John Neagle (see cat. nos. 21 and 26) is much more fully modeled, and the textures of costume and hair are more realistically rendered.

The absence of three-dimensional modeling in the face and arms of the sitter and the linear handling of her curls and other decorative details suggest that this work was painted by a self-taught artist. The Windsor chair in the background is also more modest than the furnishings usually found in academic portraits of the early nineteenth century. But it is precisely the sense of quaintness and the straightforward charm of plain portraits produced by self-taught artists that help account for their popularity among today's audiences. Modern viewers are often attracted by the artist's simple sense of color and design rather than by the historical importance or social position of the sitter.

Reference:

Mantle Fielding, *Exhibition of American Portraits, Collection of John Frederick Lewis*, exhib. cat., Philadelphia: Pennsylvania Academy of the Fine Arts, 1934, no. 99.

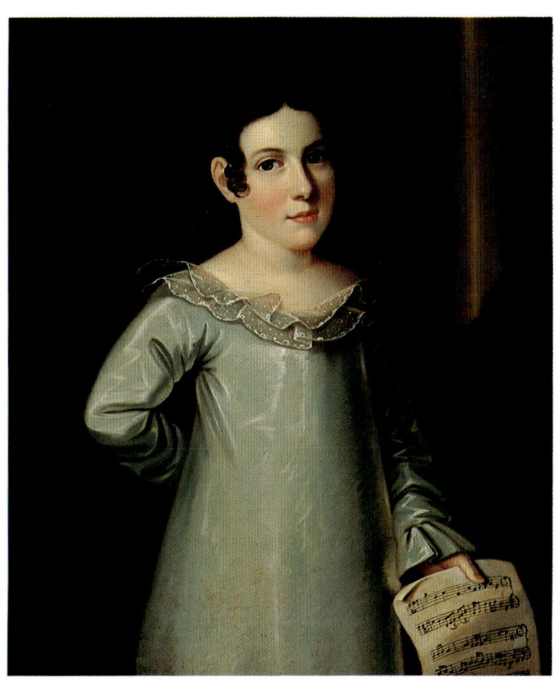

15
Unidentified Girl, 1818
Oil on canvas
30¹/8 × 24¹/4 in. (76.5 × 61.6 cm)
Gift of John Frederick Lewis, 1923.8.19

•

In the early nineteenth century, the study of music was one of the few educational pursuits open to women. The prominent display of a sheet of music in this portrait clearly conveys the sitter's interest in the subject. While her identity and exact age are unknown, her fashionable dress and hairstyle suggest a certain degree of wealth and social standing. The loose-fitting garment also reflects changing attitudes toward children's dress during this period. As childhood began to be seen as a stage of life in which play and freedom of movement were to be encouraged, dress styles for girls became simpler and less restrictive.

Francis Martin Drexel was an Austrian-born artist who came to Philadelphia in 1817 and quickly established himself as a member of the local artistic community. Among the eleven paintings that he showed the following year at the Pennsylvania Academy of the Fine Arts, eight were portraits. He continued to exhibit at the Academy until 1825, when he left for extensive travel in South America. After his return in 1830, Drexel painted few portraits, as his interest gradually turned to banking; and, in 1837, he abandoned his artistic career to become one of the city's leading financiers. Describing his own talents as a painter, Drexel wrote, "I continued to do middle well." In Philadelphia, where the competition among portrait painters was especially keen, Drexel showed foresight in turning to banking when he did. Better-known artists such as Thomas Sully (see cat. nos. 12, 16, and 29), John Neagle (see cat. nos. 21 and 26), and Henry Inman (see cat. nos. 24 and 27) surpassed him in skill and productivity. Drexel's portraits, with their directness and sense of specificity, however, are typical of the work sought after by many patrons of the middle and upper middle class who merely wanted a good likeness.

References:

Boies Penrose, "The Early Life of F. M. Drexel, 1792-1837," *Pennsylvania Magazine of History and Biography* 60 (Oct. 1936), pp. 329-357.

Francis Martin Drexel, 1792-1863, exhib. cat., Philadelphia: Drexel Museum Collection, 1976.

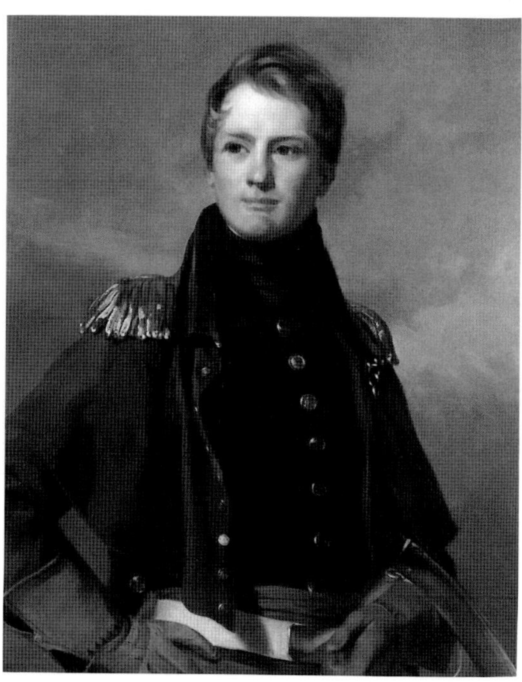

16
Major Thomas Biddle, 1818
Oil on canvas
36 1/2 × 28 1/16 in. (92.7 × 71.3 cm)
Bequest of Ann E. Biddle, 1925.8

As Thomas Sully's portrait suggests, Major Thomas Biddle (1790-1831) was a dashing figure with a romantic personal history. The son of wealthy Philadelphians, he joined the United States Army as a captain and fought in the War of 1812. He returned to Philadelphia after the war to command Fort Mifflin on the Delaware River. In 1816, he accompanied Major Stephen Long on one of the first military expeditions to Illinois; and, in 1819, Biddle traveled up the Mississippi and Missouri rivers. The following year, he settled in Saint Louis, where he remained for the rest of his life. Biddle died tragically in 1831, after a duel fought over a political disagreement with Spencer Pettis, a congressman from Missouri, who also succumbed to his wounds.

According to Sully's account book, Biddle posed several times in March and April of 1818 and paid $150 for the finished portrait. As was his custom, Sully made a preliminary sketch (private collection) to capture the general pose and the details of Biddle's uniform. The portrait must have been considered a good likeness because the painter's son, Thomas Wilcocks Sully, Jr. (1811-1847), made a copy of it for Biddle's sister Ann in 1832, after the sitter's death. The copy was once owned by the collector Thomas B. Clarke and is now in the National Gallery of Art, Washington, D. C. Sully's painting was also reproduced as an engraving by Samuel Sartain (1830-1906) for the series Eminent Philadelphians.

References:

Edward Biddle and Mantle Fielding, *The Life and Works of Thomas Sully*, Philadelphia: Wickersham Press, 1921, no. 146.

Nicholas B. Wainwright, "The Life and Death of Major Thomas Biddle," *Pennsylvania Magazine of History and Biography* 104 (July 1980), pp. 326-344.

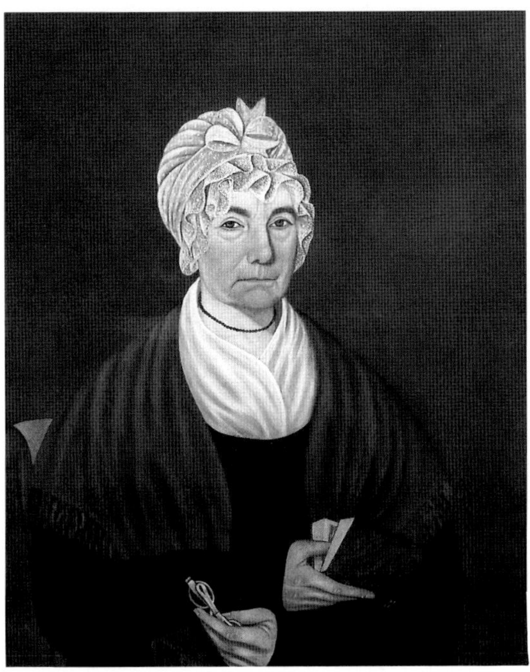

17
Unidentified Woman, ca. 1820
Oil on canvas, 33 1/8 × 27 in. (84.1 × 68.6 cm)
Bequest of David J. Grossman in honor of Mr. and Mrs. Charles S. Grossman and Mr. and Mrs. Meyer Speiser, 1979.1.11

•

The stylistic features that distinguish this portrait are the position of the sitter's crossed hands, the soft gray modeling of the folds in her shawl and scarf, and the careful delineation of the creases in her face. Similar elements appear in the portraits of a self-taught artist from central New Jersey named Micah Williams (1782-1837). Working in Monmouth County, near his home in New Brunswick, Williams produced mainly pastel portraits between 1818 and 1830. There are only two known examples in oil, one of which is a signed portrait of Solomon Avery (ca. 1820-25, Abby Aldrich Rockefeller Folk Art Center, Williamsburg, Va.). Like the woman in the Pennsylvania Academy's portrait, several of Williams's sitters are depicted with books, held partially open with a finger or a thumb. In addition, they have similarly-shaped eyes and often a furrowed brow. Until further oil paintings by Williams can be identified, however, the attribution of this portrait must remain tentative.

Reference:

American Folk Portraits, Paintings and Drawings from the Abby Aldrich Rockefeller Folk Art Center, Boston: New York Graphic Society, 1981, pp. 193-195.

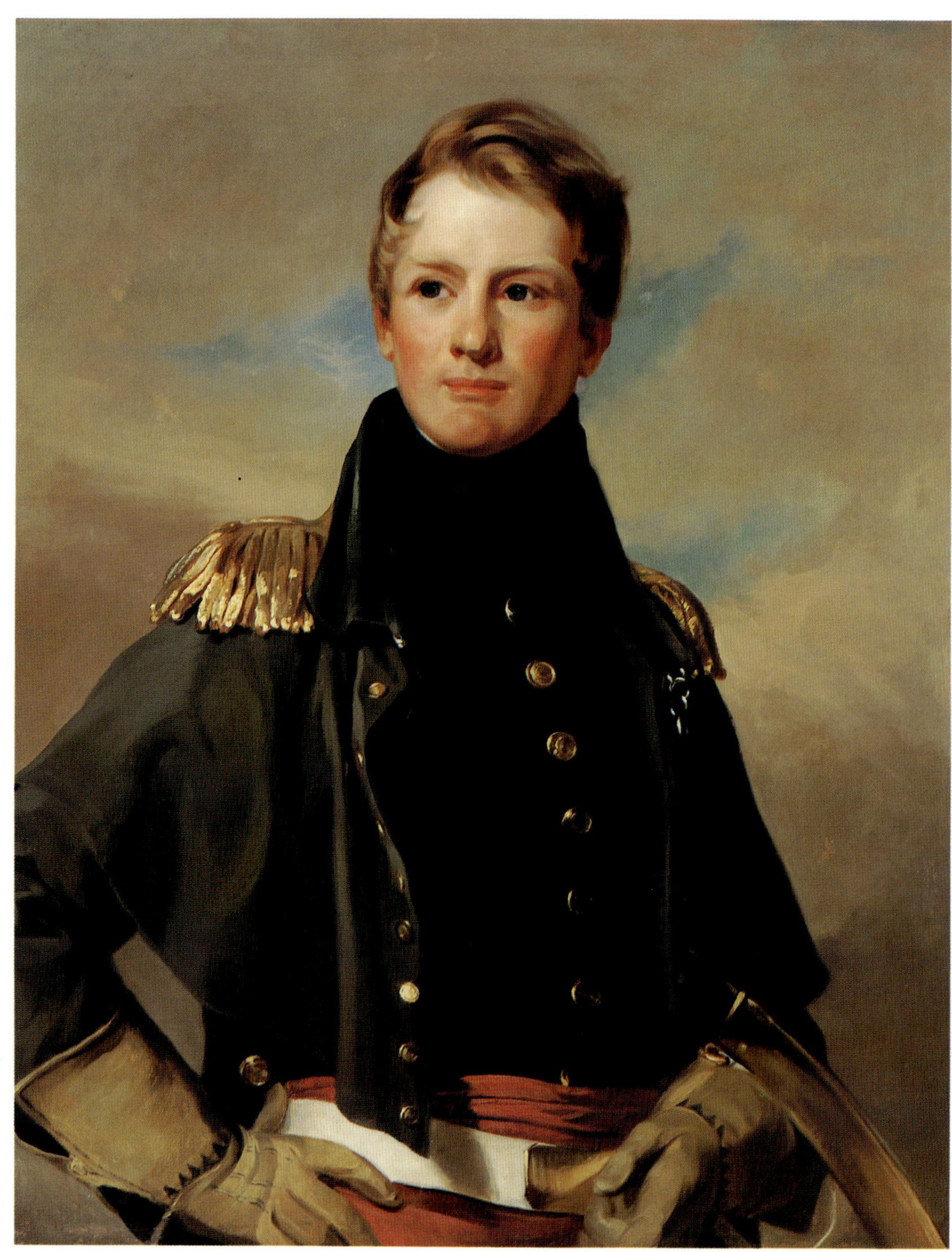

16
Major Thomas Biddle, 1818

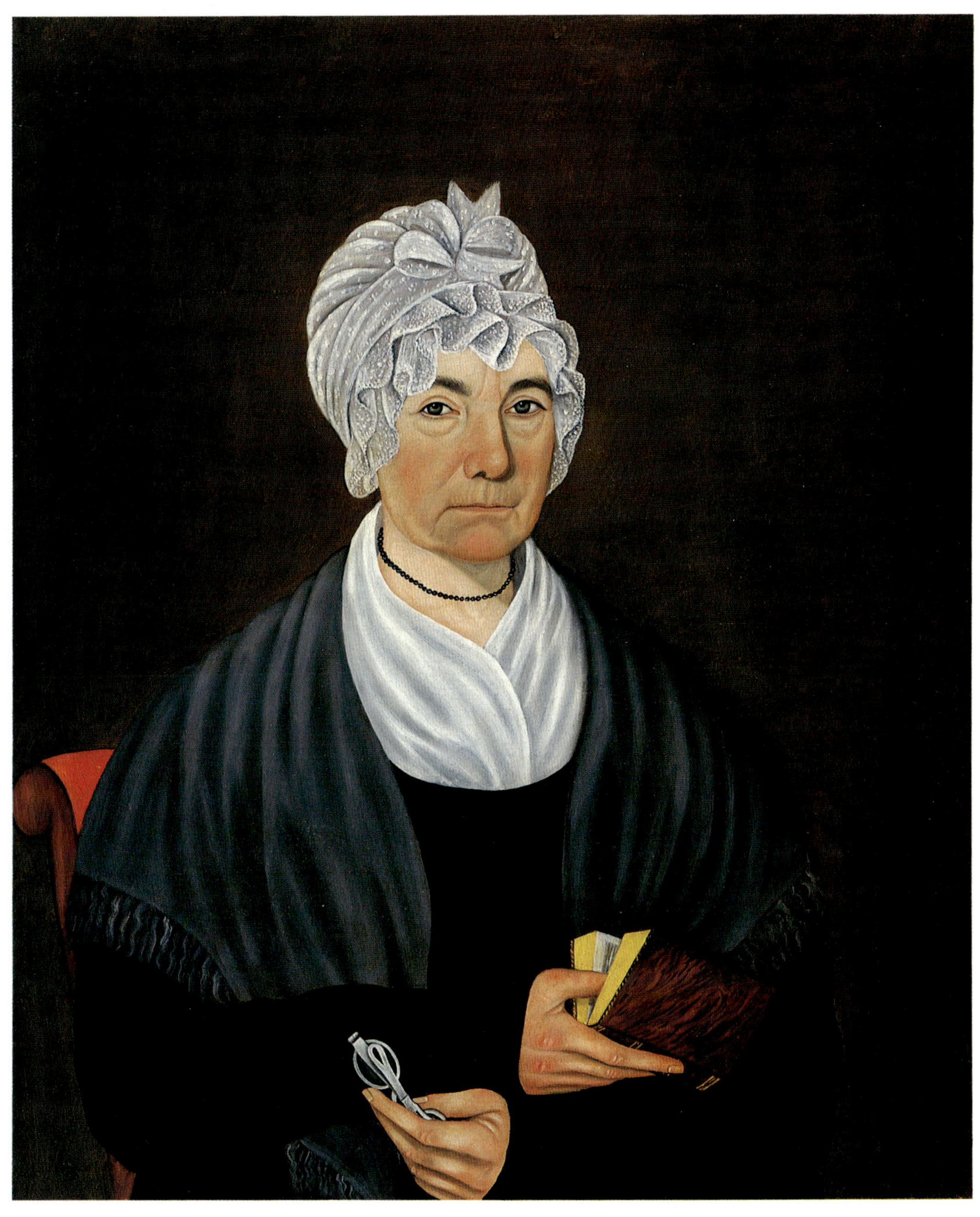

17
Unidentified Woman, ca. 1820

1800–1885

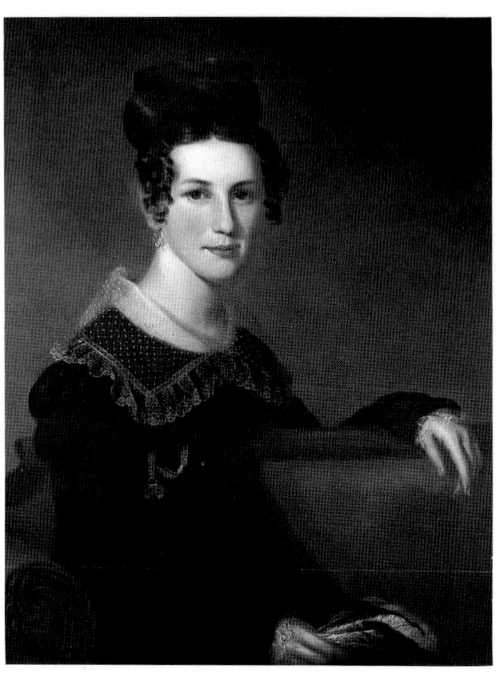

18

Anna Maria Smyth, 1821

Oil on canvas, $35^{15}/16 \times 27^{7}/16$ in. (91.3 × 69.7 cm)

Gift of Mrs. John Frederick Lewis (The John Frederick Lewis Memorial Collection), 1933.10.67

•

Like her sisters, Anna and Margaretta, Sarah Miriam Peale received her artistic training in Philadelphia from her father, James (see cat. no. 7). In the mid-1820s, she established a successful studio in Baltimore and, in the course of the next twenty years, produced over a hundred portraits. She competed for commissions with such well-known artists as Thomas Sully (see cat. nos. 12, 16, and 29), John Wesley Jarvis (see cat. no. 19), and Jacob Eichholtz (see cat. no. 23). Her clients were for the most part well-to-do Baltimore merchants and civic leaders. In the early 1840s, however, she also made trips to Washington, D.C., to paint nationally prominent politicians, such as Daniel Webster and Senators Thomas Hart Benton and Lewis F. Linn of Missouri. It may have been Linn who, in 1847, invited Peale to visit Saint Louis. She remained there for the next thirty years and continued to paint portraits and still lifes. She returned to Philadelphia to live with her two sisters in 1878.

One of the most distinctive features of Sarah Miriam Peale's portraits is her interest in decorative details. This is evident in the attention paid to the lace collar and the feathered fan in this portrait. The high degree of finish and the frontal gaze of the sitter further suggest the influence of French neoclassical portraiture. She probably learned of the style from her cousin Rembrandt Peale (see cat. no. 30), who had studied in France. The pose, hairstyle, dress, and the distinctive fob worn at the end of a gold chain in this work are almost identical to those found in another portrait, *Mrs. Isaac Avery*, also dated 1821 (private collection). According to a note in the catalogue of the Lewis collection, the sitter in the Pennsylvania Academy's portrait was the wife of a Captain Matthew J. Bernside.

References:

Mantle Fielding, *Exhibition of American Portraits, Collection of John Frederick Lewis*, exhib. cat., Philadelphia: Pennsylvania Academy of the Fine Arts, 1934, no. 140.

Wilbur H. Hunter and John Mahey, *Miss Sarah Miriam Peale, 1800-1885, Portraits and Still Lifes*, exhib. cat., Baltimore: The Peale Museum, 1967.

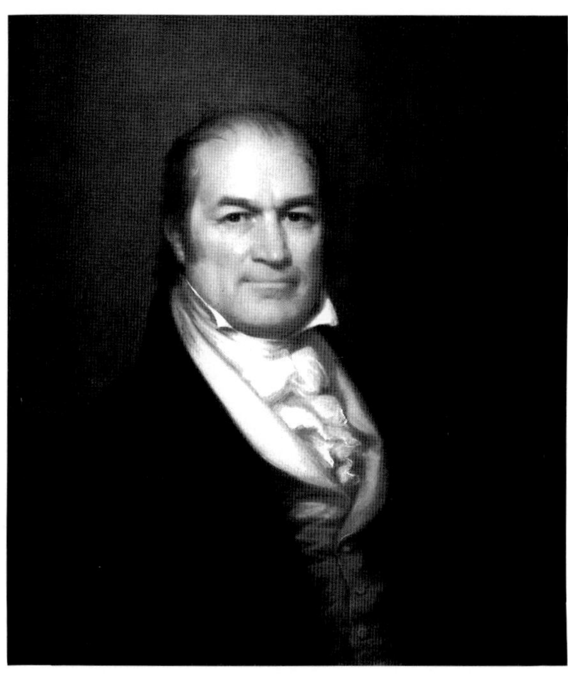

19
William Harris Crawford, 1823
Oil on canvas
30 7/16 × 25 1/8 in. (77.3 × 63.8 cm)
Gift of Charles Roberts, 1899.6

William Harris Crawford (1772-1834), a powerful senator from Georgia, served as minister to France under President James Madison and later as secretary of the treasury under President James Monroe. Seen by many as a successor to Monroe, Crawford unfortunately suffered a crippling stroke that ended his political career soon after this portrait was completed. Crawford's assured demeanor and fashionable Napoleonic hairstyle, emphasized by delicate strokes of paint and bold highlighting in this portrait, give a sense of the political power that he wielded. Jarvis's painting of Crawford was engraved by Asher B. Durand (1796-1886). Another print after the painting was included in the *National Portrait Gallery of Distinguished Americans* by James Herring and James B. Longacre (1839, vol. 4, opp. p. 1), one of the first attempts to create a compendium of portraits of national heroes. Along with Jarvis's portrait, the book contained a lengthy biography of the sitter, which described Crawford as "a man considerably above ordinary height, large, muscular, and well proportioned. His head and face were remarkably striking, and impressed the beholder at once with the belief that he must possess more than ordinary powers of intellect."

The artist John Wesley Jarvis was born in England and grew up in Philadelphia. He was apprenticed to Edward Savage and probably assisted in the production of the print after Savage's well-known painting *Washington Family at Mount Vernon* (copy, cat. no. 13). Like Savage and Charles Willson Peale (see cat. no. 6), Jarvis established his reputation by painting portraits of political and military figures, notably a series of heroes of the War of 1812 for New York's City Hall. Although he worked mainly in New York, Jarvis traveled to New Orleans in 1820 and Boston in 1822 with his apprentice Henry Inman (see cat. nos. 24 and 27) in search of commissions. Jarvis was one of the earliest artists to show contemporary portraits at the Pennsylvania Academy's annual exhibitions. Between 1811 and 1823, he exhibited fifteen works, including two that were painted for *Delaplaines's Repository of the Lives and Portraits of Distinguished American Characters* (Philadelphia, 1815-1818), one of the first books of American portraits.

References:

Harold E. Dickinson, *John Wesley Jarvis, American Painter, 1780-1840*, New York: New-York Historical Society, 1949, pp. 270-271, no. 58.

Lillian B. Miller et al., *"If Elected. . ." Unsuccessful Candidates for the Presidency*, 1796-1968, exhib. cat., Washington, D. C.: National Portrait Gallery, 1972, pp. 81-83.

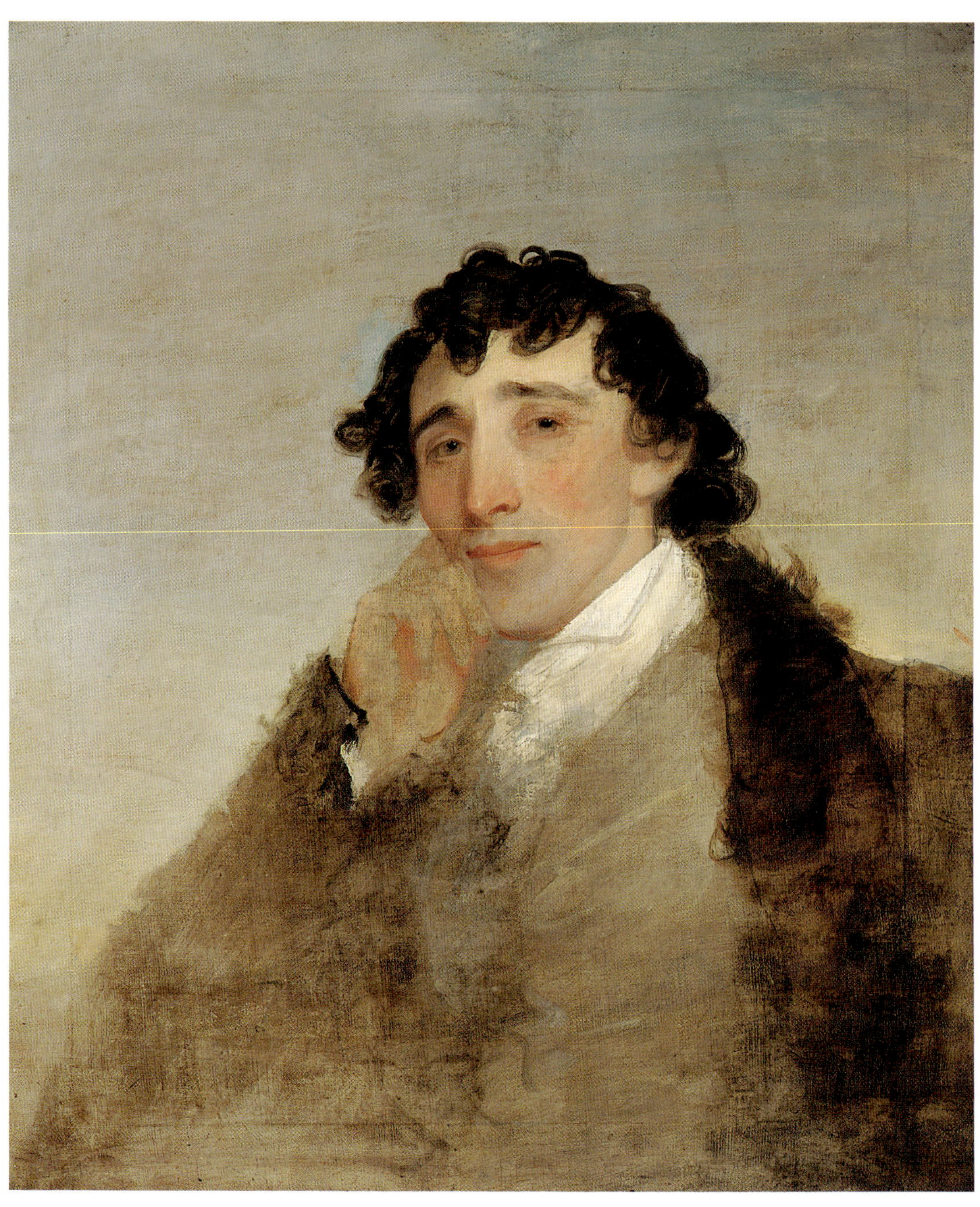

20
Peter Grayson, 1827

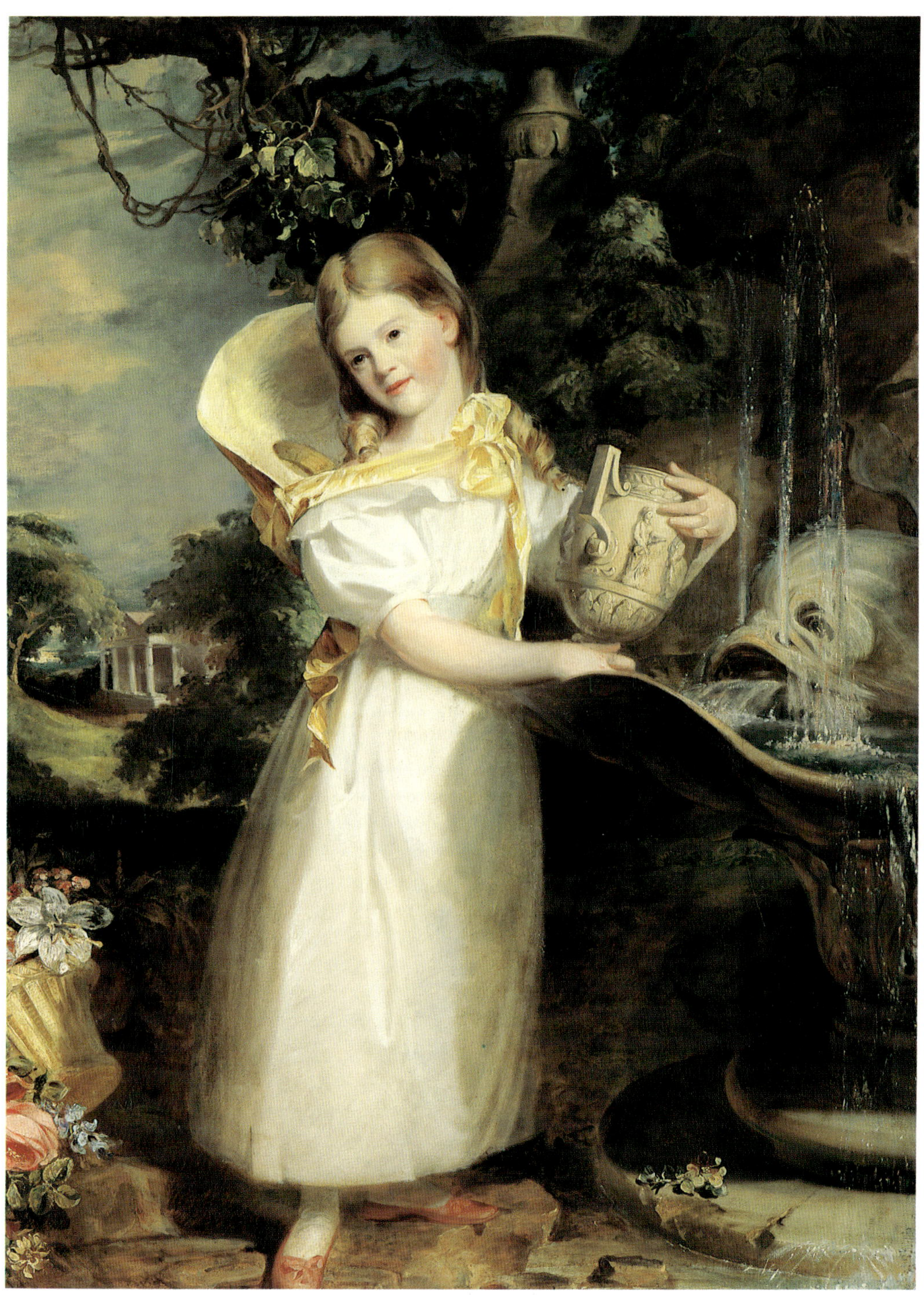

21
Matilda Washington Dawson, 1829

1788–1827

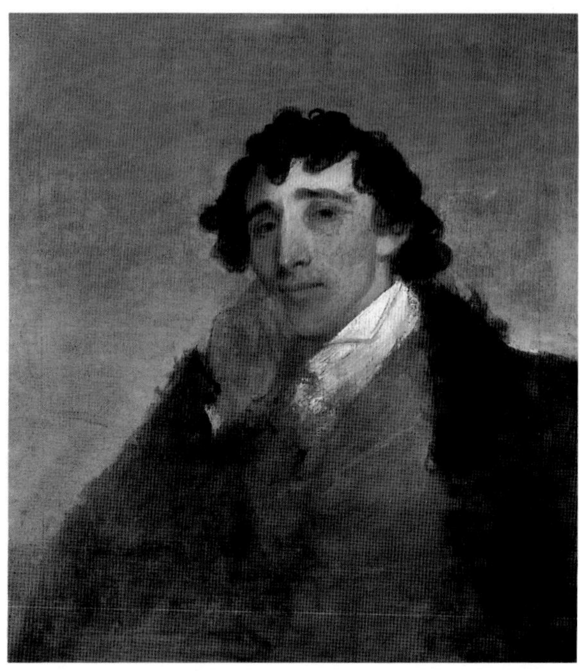

20
Peter Grayson, 1827
Oil on canvas
30 × 25 in. (76.2 × 63.5 cm)
Gift of Mrs. Sarah B. Menefee, 1897.1

In 1816, Matthew Harris Jouett, a young portrait painter from Kentucky, traveled to Boston in search of instruction. He became a favorite student of Gilbert Stuart (see cat. nos. 1-3) and took detailed notes on Stuart's theories and techniques of portrait painting. At the time, Stuart's sketch for his famous Athenaeum head of George Washington was in his studio; and it is likely that Jouett made copies that he took back to Kentucky. The unfinished portrait of Peter Grayson provides the viewer with an opportunity to see how Jouett applied the lessons that he had learned from Stuart, who stressed the importance of the preliminary sketch: "In the commencement of all portraits, the first idea is an indistinct mass of light and shadows, or the character of the person as seen in the heel of the evening in the grey of the morning, or at a distance too great to discriminate features with exactness" ("Notes Taken by M. H. Jouett while in Boston from Conve[r]sations on painting with Gilbert Stuart Esqr," 1816, reprinted in Floyd [1968], p. 169).

Several of his contemporaries, including John Neagle (see cat. nos. 21 and 26) and George P. A. Healy (see cat. no. 31), regarded Jouett as the best portraitist west of the Appalachian Mountains. After his return to Kentucky, Jouett set up a portrait studio in Lexington. He traveled down the Mississippi River to Louisville, Natchez, and New Orleans during the winter months in search of commissions. His clients seemed to prefer bust-length portraits, for which he generally charged fifty dollars. In a letter to Thomas Sully (see cat. nos. 12, 16, and 29), written in November of 1822, Jouett complained of difficulty in supporting his growing family and of a longing to visit Philadelphia to see "good pictures" to stimulate his own artistic endeavors. The sitter in this portrait, Peter Grayson (ca. 1793-1838), was a lawyer and a close friend of the artist. The portrait was left unfinished in his studio when Jouett died suddenly at the age of thirty-nine. Grayson, moved by the loss of his friend, wrote a sentimental poem about his passing.

References:

William Barrow Floyd, *Jouett-Bush-Frazer, Early Kentucky Artists*, Lexington, privately printed, 1968, pp. 11-81 and 169-177.

———, *Matthew Harris Jouett, Portraits of the Ante-Bellum South*, exhib. cat., Lexington: Mitchell Fine Arts Center, Transylvania University, 1980, no. 51.

1796–1865

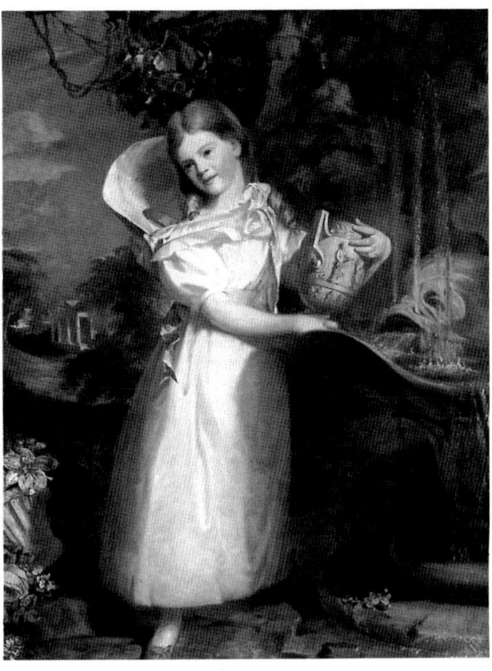

21

Matilda Washington Dawson, 1829

Oil on canvas

$56^3/_8 \times 40^7/_8$ in. (143.2 × 103.8 cm)

Bequest of General Joseph Ripley Chandler Ward, 1931.14

•

Although nothing is known about the sitter, the elaborate background in this portrait suggests a great deal about her social status and about contemporary artistic taste. Flanked by flowers and shrubs in a neoclassical setting, the sitter appears to be a contemporary incarnation of the Greek goddess Flora. Neagle was noted for the elaborately detailed backgrounds in his portraits and, in this work, the portico of the house in the distance, the vase held by the girl, and the garden ornaments that surround her all allude to the classical world. Such references were especially fashionable in Philadelphia during the second quarter of the nineteenth century, when the Greek Revival style was at the height of its popularity. This style first manifested itself in architecture and the decorative arts but soon had an impact on painting as well.

During the late eighteenth and early nineteenth centuries, several of Philadelphia's prominent families built neoclassical houses on large estates along the banks of nearby rivers. In this painting, the picturesque garden setting with the classical portico and the body of water beyond evokes the grandeur of well-known houses, such as the Woodlands. Completed in 1789 near Gray's Ferry on the Schuylkill, it had a similar four-columned porch and a large garden noted for luxuriant plantings and a spring-fed grotto. Several of Neagle's patrons were founding members of the Pennsylvania Horticultural Society in 1827, and they would have especially appreciated this use of a garden setting.

References:

Robert W. Torchia, *John Neagle: Philadelphia Portrait Painter*, exhib. cat., Philadelphia: Historical Society of Pennsylvania, 1989, no. 17.

Richard J. Betts, "The Woodlands," *Winterthur Portfolio* 14 (Autumn 1979), pp. 213-234.

1792–1866

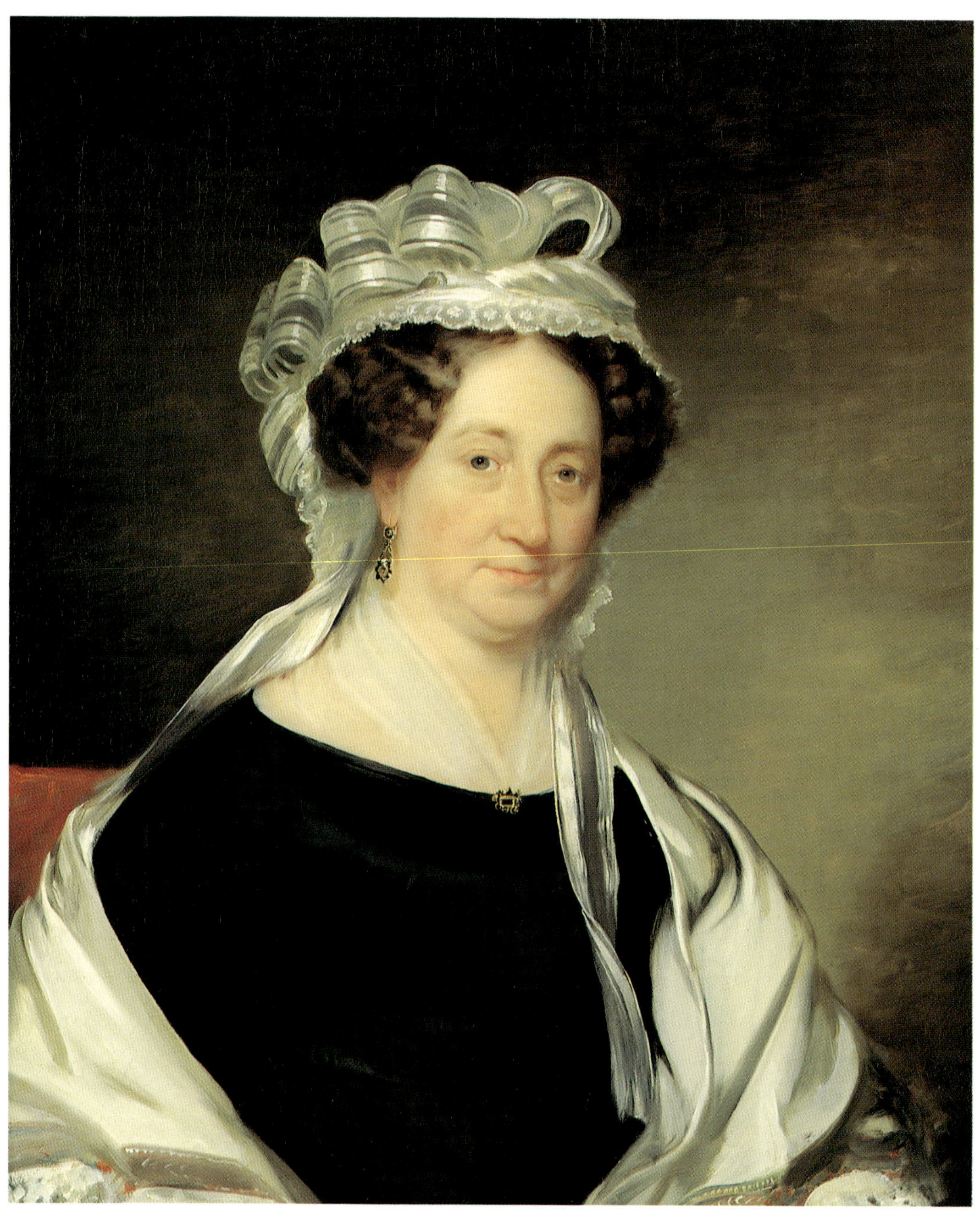

22
Mrs. William Lorman, ca. 1830

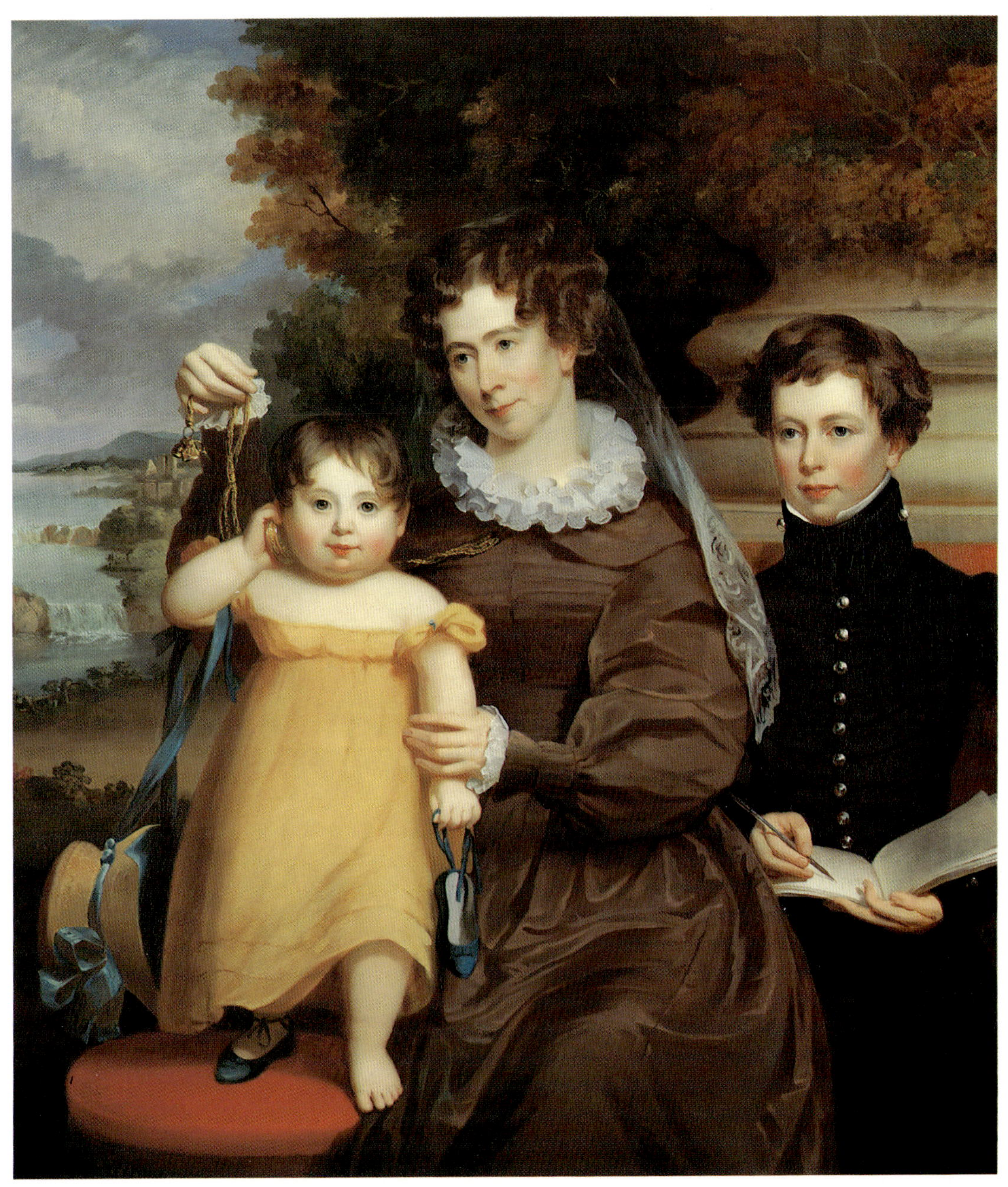

23
Mrs. Victor René Value, Her Daughter Victoria Matilda, and Her Stepson Jesse René, ca. 1830

Chester Harding

1792–1866

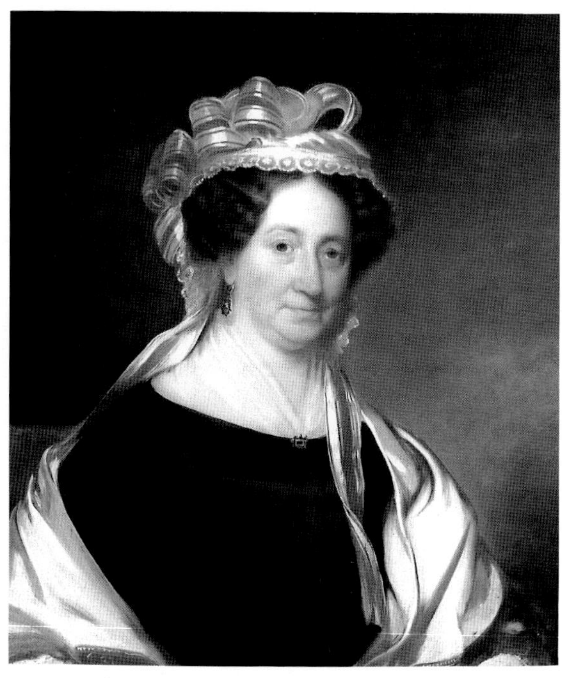

22

MRS. WILLIAM LORMAN, ca. 1830
Oil on canvas
30 × 24⅞ in. (76.2 × 63.2 cm)
Bequest of Mrs. Eleanor F. T. Conner, 1921.10.1

•

Chester Harding was inspired to take up a career as an artist when he saw the work of an unidentified itinerant portrait painter. Harding's earliest portraits show the influence of Matthew Harris Jouett (see cat. no. 20), whom he encountered while living in Kentucky. Although Harding was essentially self-taught, he was not unaware of the academic tradition in portraiture. He recounted in his memoirs that he spent the winter of 1819-20 in Philadelphia, "devoting time entirely to drawing in the [Pennsylvania] Academy, and studying the best pictures, practicing at the same time with the brush." At the Pennsylvania Academy, Harding also would have found Thomas Sully's portrait of George Frederick Cooke (cat. no. 12) and Gilbert Stuart's Lansdowne portrait of George Washington, 1796—two well-known American paintings that followed the grand manner of eighteenth-century British art.

In 1823, Harding went to England for further study. While in London, he made many important contacts with both English artists and American patrons. He was especially impressed with Sir Thomas Lawrence, whose loose handling of paint and freer effects of color reinforced the painterly approach that Harding had already observed in the work of Stuart and Sully. When Harding returned to the United States in 1826, he quickly established himself as a portraitist of political figures and of the upper middle class. Although he lived in Springfield, Massachusetts, Harding kept a studio in Boston and spent a great deal of time traveling to cities on the East Coast and in the Midwest for portrait commissions.

Harding's portrait of Mrs. William Lorman (née Mary Fulford in 1770) was probably executed in Baltimore, where she lived. Her husband was a prominent merchant and banker and a founding director of the Baltimore Gas Company and the Baltimore and Ohio Railroad. A portrait by Harding of William Lorman, also painted about 1830, is in the Pennsylvania Academy's collection. Neither portrait idealizes its subject. Both are shown with the accumulated wrinkles and double chins of old age. In Mrs. Lorman's portrait, the only embellishments are the ribbons and lace of her cap and the sparkling jewelry.

References:

Chester Harding, *My Egotistigraphy*, Cambridge: John Wilson and Son, 1866.

Leah Lipton, *A Truthful Likeness, Chester Harding and His Portraits*, exhib. cat., Washington, D. C.: National Portrait Gallery, 1985, p. 167.

1776–1842

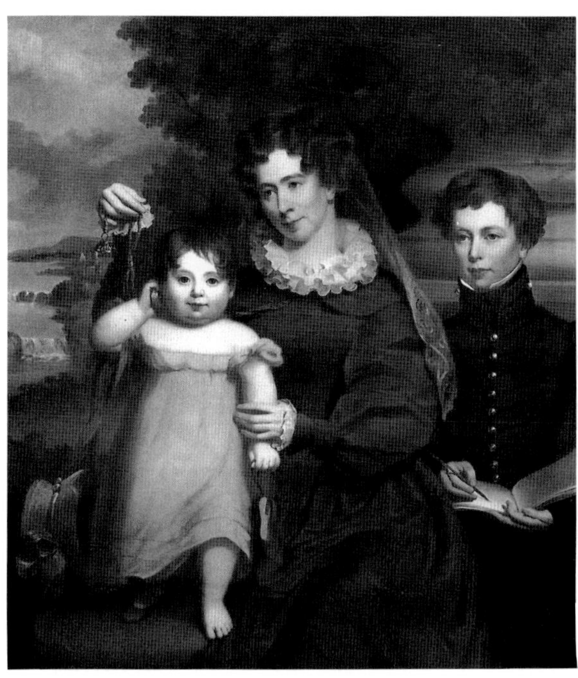

23

MRS. VICTOR RENÉ VALUE, HER DAUGHTER VICTORIA MATILDA, AND HER STEPSON JESSE RENÉ, ca. 1830
Oil on canvas, $52^7/_8 \times 45$ in. (134.2 × 114.3 cm)
Gift of Mrs. Charles E. Dunbar, 1986.40

This engaging family portrait provides important insights into nineteenth-century attitudes toward childhood. The younger child is listening to a pocket watch, dangling from a chain held by the mother. Although fashionably dressed, the toddler has one shoe missing, as a sign of mischievousness. Her older brother seems more serious. He wears a military uniform and holds a pen and notebook. By distinguishing the dress, demeanor, and gender roles of these two children, the painting suggests that the early years of childhood are meant for play but that, as a child grows older, education and duty become more important, especially for boys. The watch and the introspective gaze of the mother serve as poignant reminders that childhood years will pass quickly. The emphasis on education in the portrait also relates to the profession of the children's father, Victor Value. He was a teacher of French and, for a time, the proprietor of a school on Washington Square in Philadelphia, where Jacob Eichholtz sent his own daughter in 1834. Thomas Sully painted a portrait of Victor Value and his other daughter, Charlotte (1828, Museum of Fine Arts, Boston).

Eichholtz was a self-taught artist from Lancaster, Pennsylvania, who sought advice on portrait painting from both Gilbert Stuart (see cat. nos. 1-3) and Thomas Sully (see cat. nos. 12, 16, and 29). After an itinerant career in Lancaster, Harrisburg, and Baltimore, Eichholtz settled in Philadelphia about 1823 and participated frequently in the annual exhibitions of the Pennsylvania Academy of the Fine Arts. Over the next decade, he built a steady business as a portrait painter. A measure of his success is the price paid for this portrait, $135, which at the time was a considerable sum of money for a portrait commission (The better known Sully charged $175 for his portrait of Victor Value). This relatively high price reflects the complexity of Eichholtz's composition, which included multiple figures, as well as the base of a classical column and a generic landscape in the background. This type of portrait, known as a conversation piece, was derived from eighteenth-century English painting, where it was usually associated with wealthy patrons. It lent an air of aristocratic tradition to Eichholtz's middle-class sitters.

References:

M. and M. Karolik Collection of American Paintings, 1815-1865, Boston: Museum of Fine Arts, 1949, no. 216.

Rebecca J. Beal, *Jacob Eichholtz*, 1776-1842, Philadelphia: Historical Society of Pennsylvania, 1969, no. 839.

1801–1846

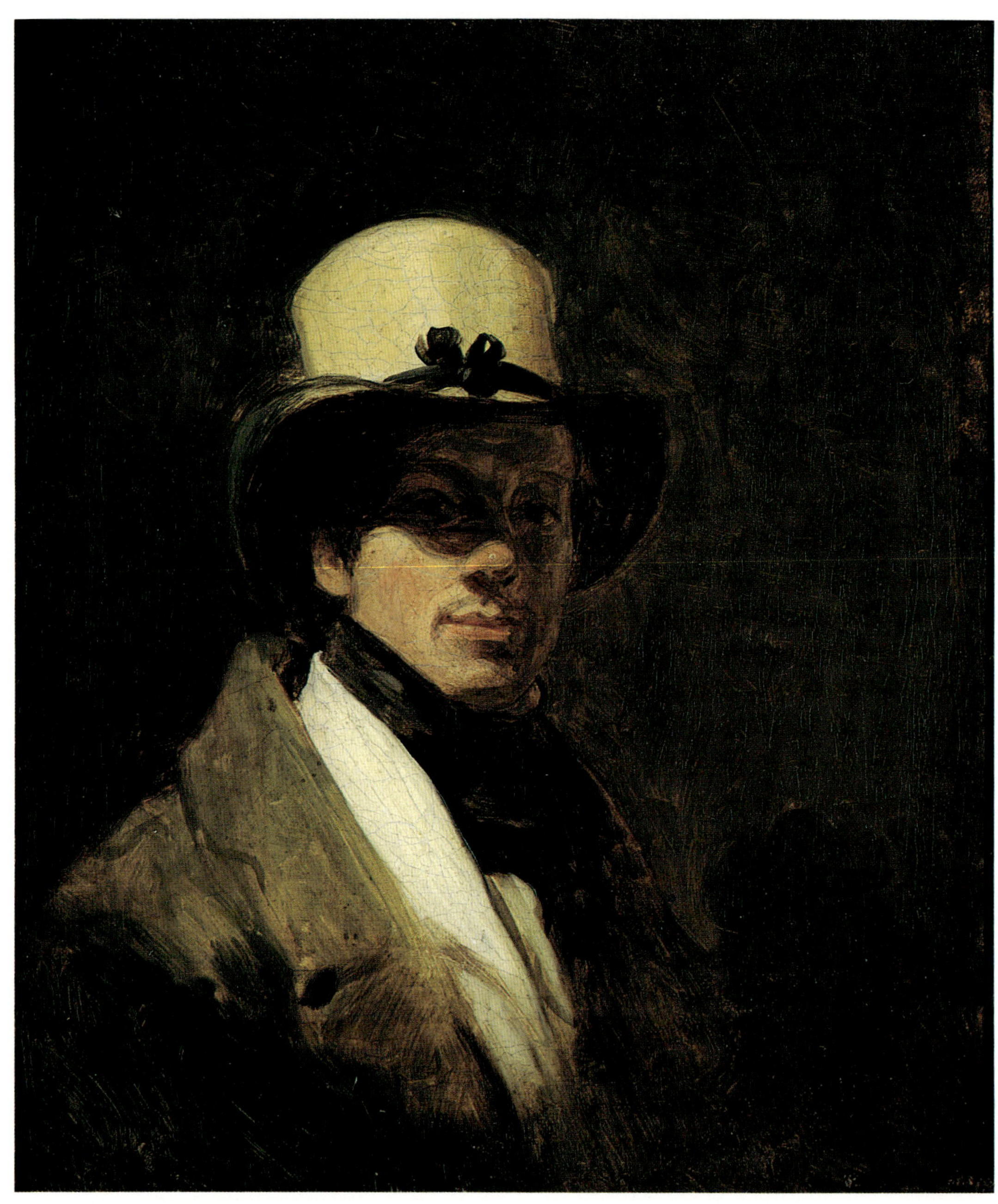

24
Self-Portrait, 1834

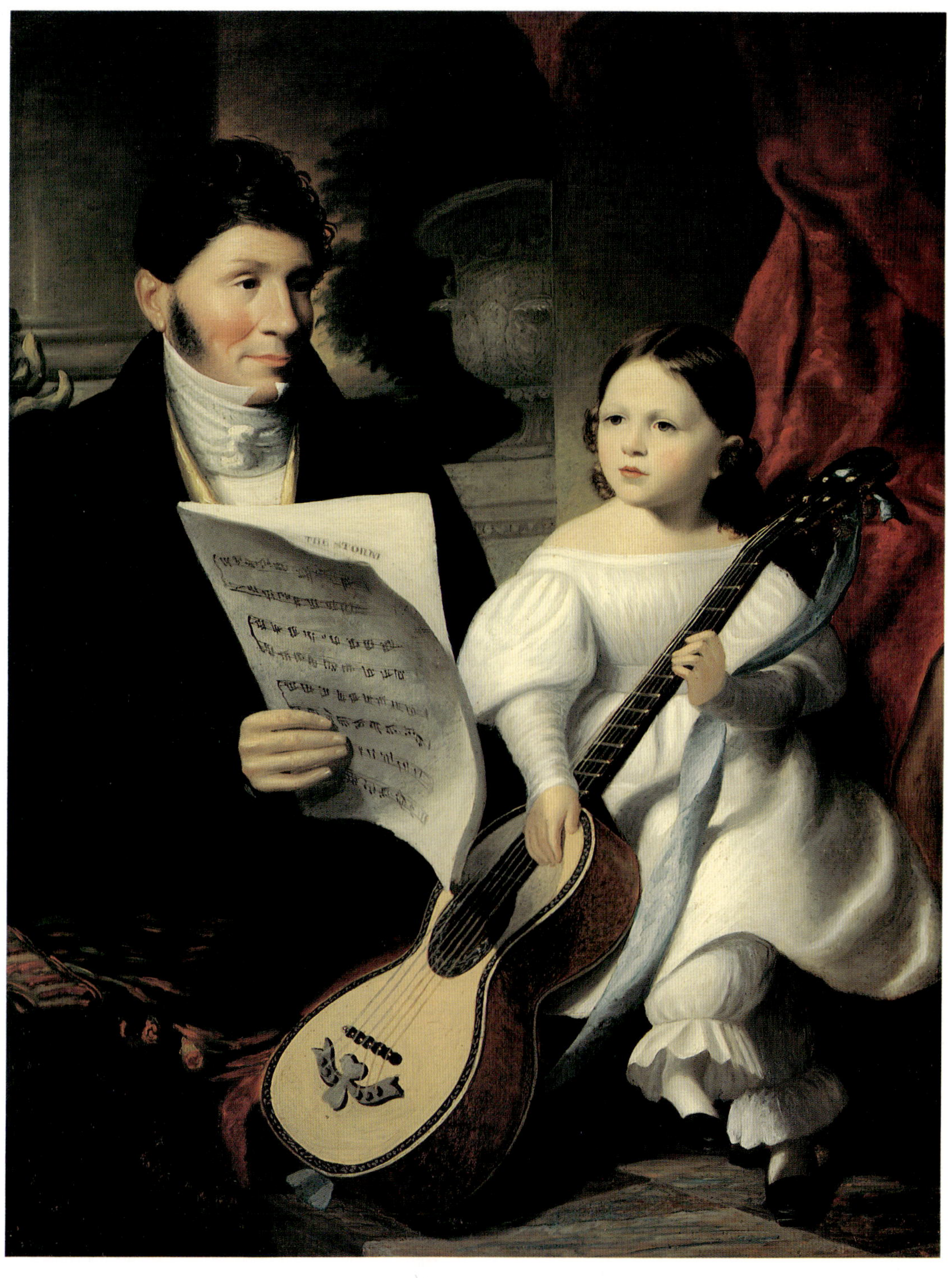

25
The Music Master, ca. 1835

1801–1846

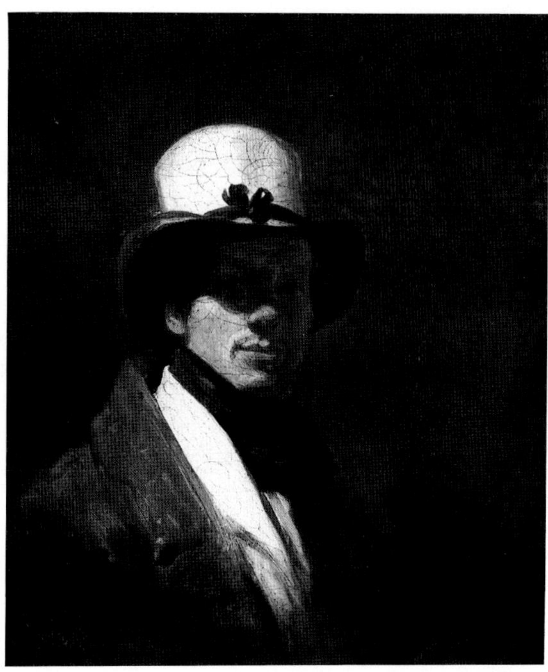

24
SELF-PORTRAIT, 1834
Oil on canvas
12¹/16 × 10¹/16 in. (30.6 × 25.6 cm)
Bequest of Cephas G. Childs, 1871.1.1

Henry Inman was one of New York's leading portrait painters, but he spent the years between 1831 and 1834 working in the Philadelphia area, where this portrait was executed. The Philadelphia artist John Sartain (1808–1897) reported that Inman finished the painting in one sitting as a demonstration to three young students. The loose handling of paint, therefore, was as much the result of rapid execution as of style. The dramatic shadows on Inman's face and the highlight on his tall straw hat recall elements of Thomas Sully's romantic portraits, such as *The Torn Hat* (1820, Museum of Fine Arts, Boston) and *The Student* (1839, Metropolitan Museum of Art, New York). The common source for this use of chiaroscuro, or strong highlighting, may well have been the portraits of Rembrandt, one of which both Sully and Inman would have known through their patron, Edward L. Carey. Carey was related by marriage to Anna Leslie, who exhibited her copy (present location unknown) of a Rembrandt self-portrait at the Pennsylvania Academy of the Fine Arts in 1826.

Inman began his portrait career in 1814 as an apprentice to John Wesley Jarvis (see cat. no. 19), a New York painter whose loose handling of paint and use of bright highlights influenced his young student. By the late 1820s, Inman had succeeded Jarvis as the most fashionable portraitist in the city. Like Sully, Inman produced numerous portraits of popular actors. He had many Philadelphia patrons and was a frequent participant in the annual exhibitions at the Pennsylvania Academy. Inman served on the board of directors of the Academy in 1834. A versatile artist, he was highly regarded for miniatures, landscapes, genre paintings, and innovative lithographic prints.

References:

Theodore Bolton, "Henry Inman, an Account of his Life," *Art Quarterly* 3 (Autumn 1940), pp. 353-374.

Ann C. Van Devanter et al., *American Self-Portraits*, 1670-1973, exhib. cat., New York: E. P. Dutton for International Exhibitions Foundation, 1974, no. 21.

William H. Gerdts and Carrie Rebora, *The Art of Henry Inman*, exhib. cat., Washington, D. C.: National Portrait Gallery, 1987, no. 93.

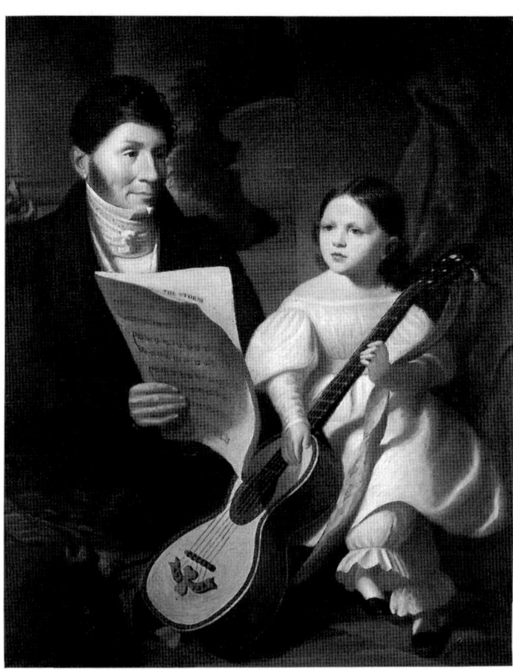

25
The Music Master, ca. 1835
Oil on canvas, 48×36 in. (121.9×91.4 cm)
Gift of Mrs. John Frederick Lewis (The John Frederick Lewis Memorial Collection), 1933.10.90

•

The most popular stringed instrument in the early nineteenth century was the Spanish guitar. Although the child in this portrait seems too young to play the large guitar that she holds, her attention is fixed on the sheet of music, entitled "The Storm," held by an elegantly clad gentleman. The title is typical of the kind of romantic music prevalent in both the United States and Europe in this period. While the names of the sitters are unknown, their roles as teacher and pupil are easily grasped. The elevated position of music among the arts is emphasized by the grand manner of this portrait. The use of background elements such as the crimson drapery, the base of a classical column, and the garden urn derived from European precedents. But the sharply rendered features of the sitters and their rather awkwardly painted hands suggest the work of an American artist who, although largely self-taught, followed academic formulas.

This portrait was attributed to Rembrandt Peale (see cat. no. 30) when it was acquired with other works in the Lewis collection in 1933. Stylistically, however, it seems more like the work of one of his contemporaries, perhaps the Portuguese-born Manuel Joachim de Franca (1808-1865). De Franca settled in Philadelphia about 1830 and exhibited both history paintings and portraits at the Pennsylvania Academy until 1853. He was a member of the Artists' Fund Society, along with more prominent painters such as Thomas Sully (see cat. nos. 12, 16, and 29) and John Neagle (see cat. nos. 21 and 26), who also tended to embellish children's portraits with elaborate backdrops. By 1847, de Franca had moved to Saint Louis, where he remained until his death.

References:

Mantle Fielding, *Exhibition of American Portraits, Collection of John Frederick Lewis*, exhib. cat., Philadelphia: Pennsylvania Academy of the Fine Arts, 1934, no. 45.

Karen McCoskey Goering, "Manuel de Franca: St. Louis Portrait Painter," *Gateway Heritage* 3 (Winter 1982-83), pp. 30-35.

H. Nicholas B. Clark, "American Musical Paintings, 1770-1865," in *The Art of Music, American Paintings and Musical Instruments, 1770-1910*, exhib. cat., Clinton, N. Y.: Fred L. Emerson Gallery, Hamilton College, 1984, pp. 31-50.

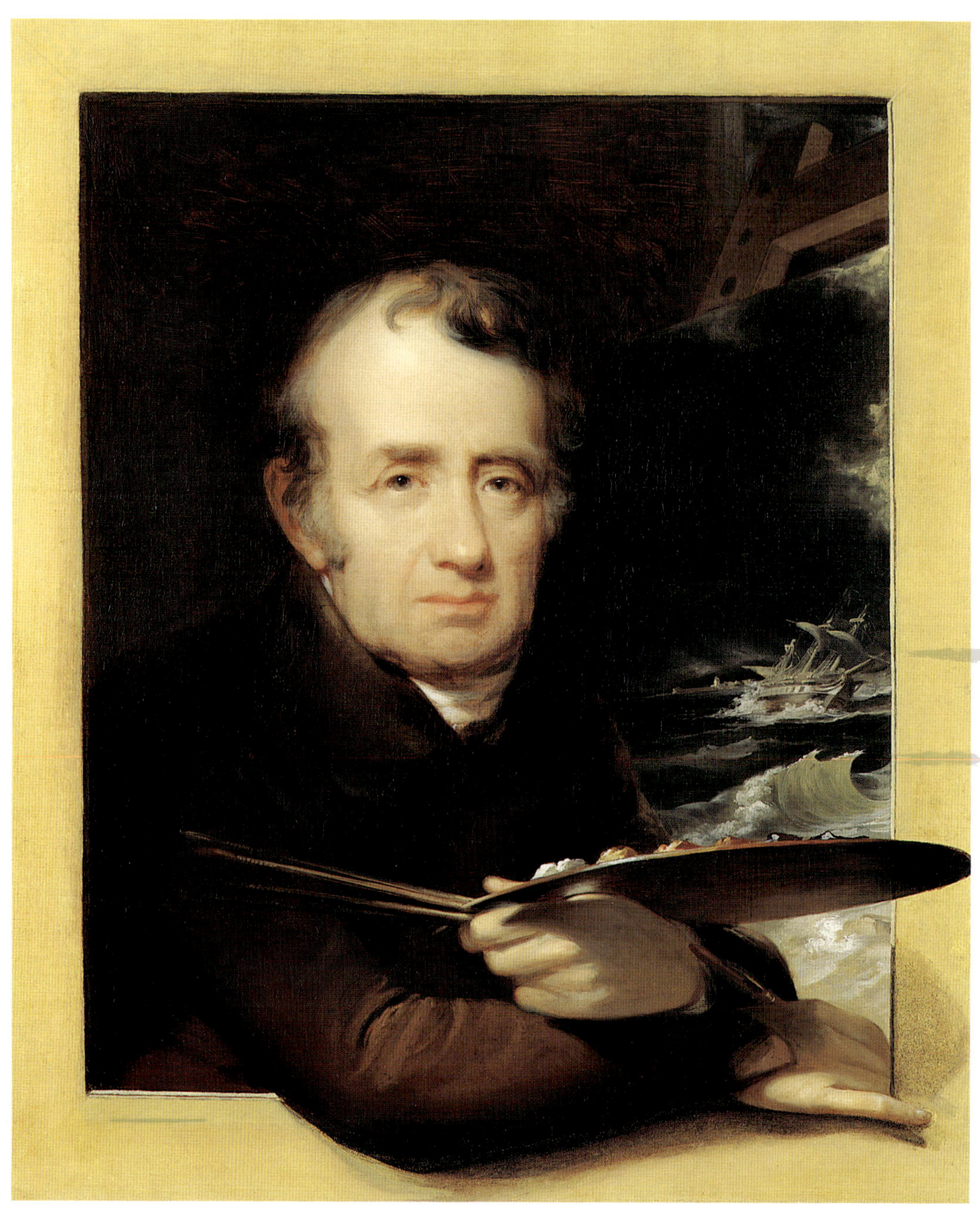

26
The Studious Artist, 1836

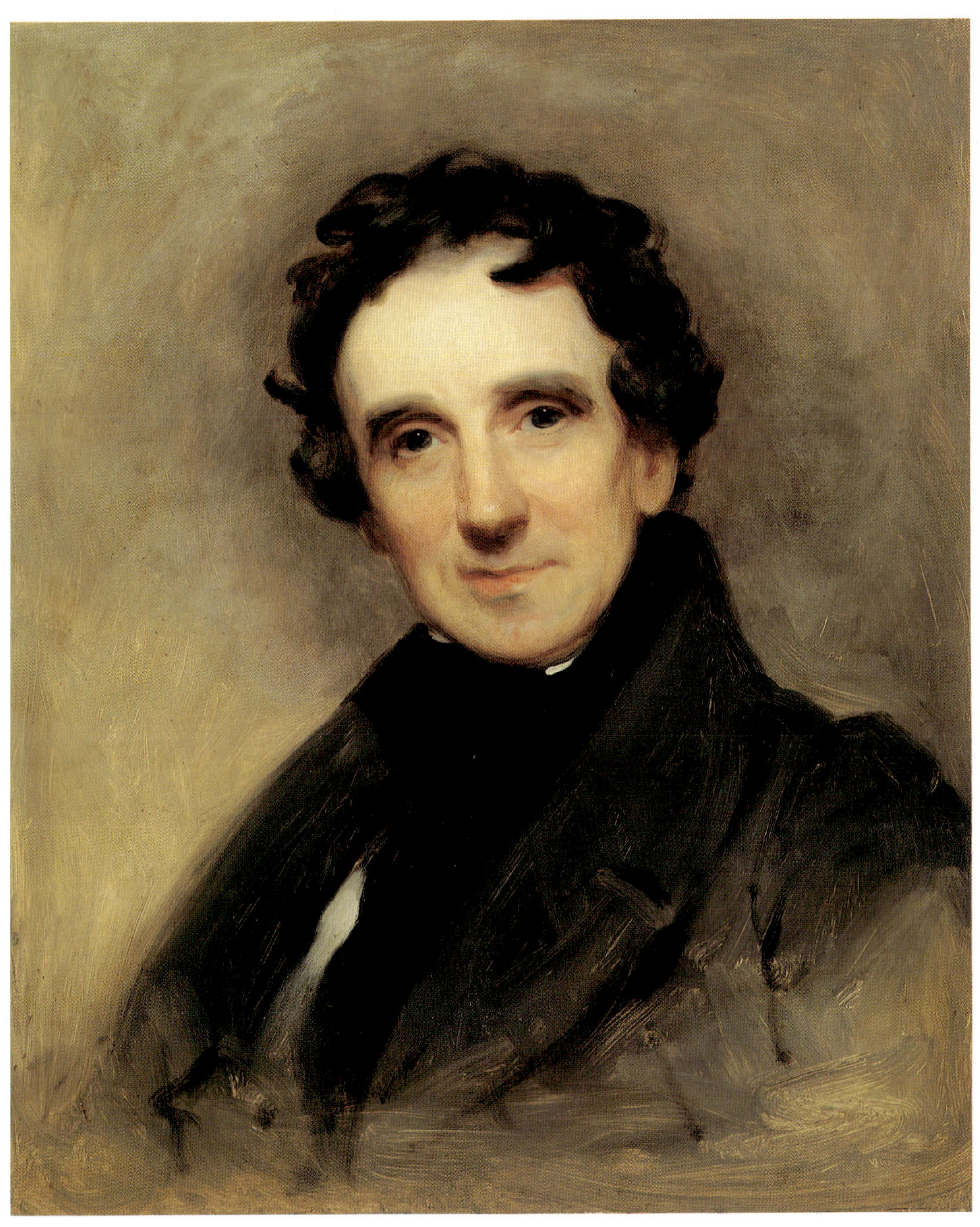

27
Thomas Sully, 1837

1796–1865

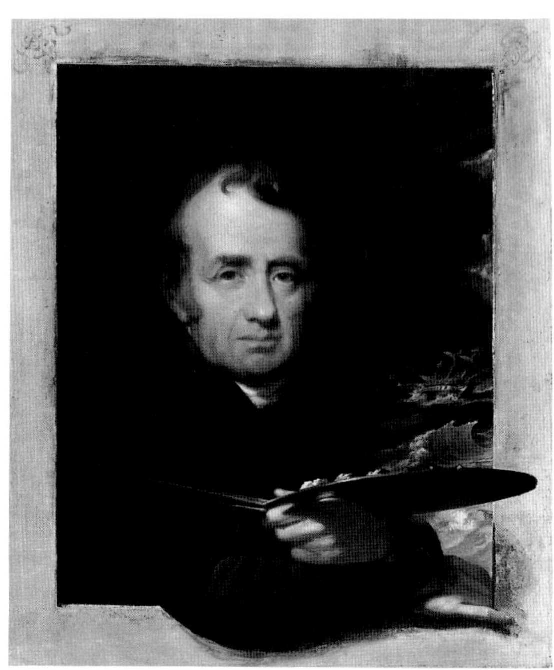

26

THE STUDIOUS ARTIST, 1836

Oil on canvas

30 1/8 × 25 1/16 in. (76.5 × 63.7 cm)

Gift of John Frederick Lewis, 1922.1.3

•

This is a portrait of John Neagle's good friend, the marine painter Thomas Birch (1779-1851). With Neagle and several other Philadelphia portraitists, including Thomas Sully (see cat. nos. 12, 16, and 29), Emanuel Leutze (see cat. no. 35), and James B. Longacre, Birch was a member of the Artists' Fund Society. Founded by Philadelphia artists to promote their work among local patrons, this group was especially keen to establish a strong regional identity. Neagle's portrait of Birch appears to have been executed as a kind of showpiece for the society, a tour-de-force of both realistic portraiture and romantic seascape. It included a trompe l'oeil frame that was originally gold-leafed. The artist's elbow and his palette appear to protrude beyond this fake frame into the viewer's space. Further complicating the spatial arrangement of the image is the painting within the painting, a seascape that sits on an easel in the background. Similar motifs can be traced to European engravings of artists' portraits of the seventeenth and eighteenth centuries.

Neagle's unusual portrait generated a great deal of controversy in the popular press when it was first shown, in 1837, at an exhibition of the Artists' Fund Society at the Pennsylvania Academy of the Fine Arts. The attack was led by the landscape painter Joshua Shaw (1776/77-1860), who questioned Neagle's skills in drawing and proportion. In the end, however, most critics were impressed with the portrait; and its notoriety helped to affirm Neagle's position as one of Philadelphia's leading portrait painters.

Reference:

Robert W. Torchia, *John Neagle: Philadelphia Portrait Painter*, exhib. cat., Philadelphia: Historical Society of Pennsylvania, 1989, pp. 62-66.

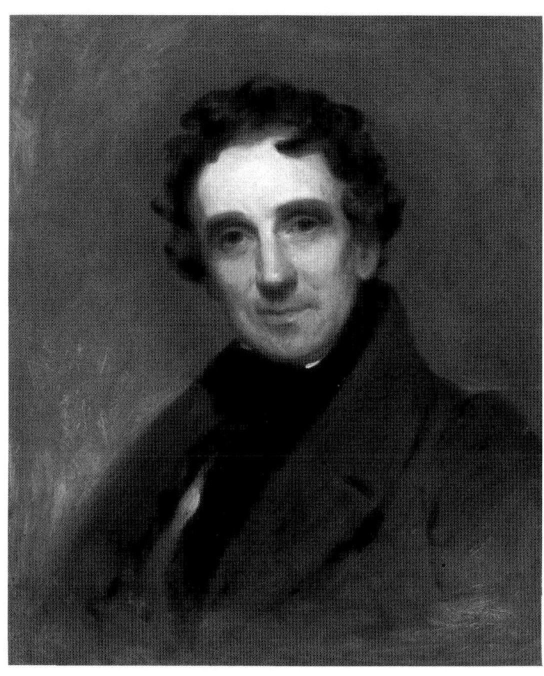

27
Thomas Sully, 1837
Oil on academy board
$23^{15}/_{16} \times 19^{13}/_{16}$ in. (60.7 × 50.3 cm)
Gift of Blanche Sully, 1891.6

Along with Thomas Sully, Henry Inman was often referred to as "the American Lawrence," a reference to Sir Thomas Lawrence, one of the leading British portraitists of the period. These three artists shared certain stylistic traits, especially the fluid handling of paint and use of rich colors. The freely applied paint in Inman's portrait of Sully precipitated a great controversy among local artists and critics when the painting was shown in the Artists' Fund Society's exhibition at the Pennsylvania Academy of the Fine Arts in 1837. At that time, New York artists like Inman were beginning to overtake Philadelphia artists in terms of popularity. Inman, especially, was viewed as a threat to the Philadelphia portrait trade; and several letters to Philadelphia newspapers focused their complaints on his portrait of Sully. Said to have been executed in just three brief sittings, it was faulted for its sketchy, unfinished state. Furthermore, the critics complained that it made the sitter look ten years older than he was. By way of contrast, one writer praised John Neagle's portrait of the artist Thomas Birch (*The Studious Artist*, cat. no. 26) for its accurate detail and the convincing seascape in the background.

These attacks on Inman's portrait may have been politically motivated, because Inman, a Democrat, had antagonized local supporters of the more conservative Whig party. Such criticism also suggests how competitive the business of portrait painting had become in Philadelphia by the mid-nineteenth century.

References:

William H. Gerdts and Carrie Rebora, *The Art of Henry Inman*, exhib. cat., Washington, D. C.: National Portrait Gallery, 1987, no. 48.

Robert W. Torchia, *John Neagle: Philadelphia Portrait Painter*, exhib. cat., Philadelphia: Historical Society of Pennsylvania, 1989, pp. 62-66.

1812–1868

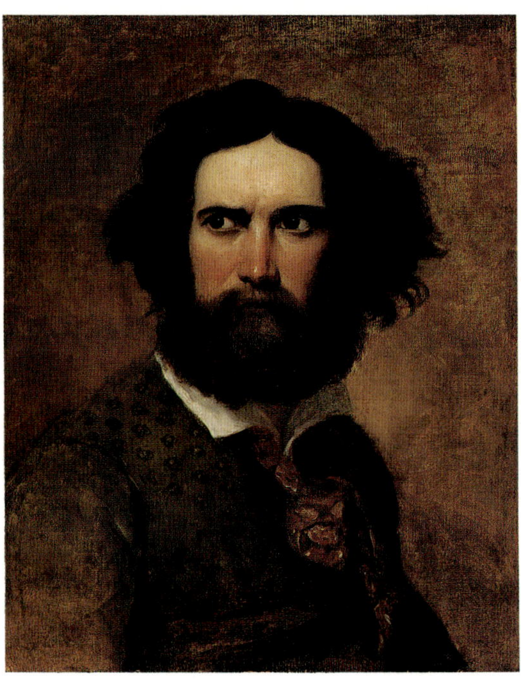

28

Self-Portrait, ca. 1840

Oil on canvas, mounted on masonite, 24⅝ × 19¹¹⁄₁₆ in. (62.5 × 50 cm)
Gift of Mrs. John Frederick Lewis (The John Frederick Lewis Memorial Collection), 1933.10.17

•

Charles Loring Elliott produced several self-portraits over the course of his career as a portraitist. This is the most romantic, with its emphasis on his unkempt hair, casual attire, and piercing gaze, which probably came from staring into a mirror in order to capture the likeness. Other portraits of Elliott also draw attention, with dramatic highlights, to his high forehead. The influence of Rembrandt is suggested by Elliott's interest in self-portraiture and his preoccupation with chiaroscuro. These strong contrasts of light and dark, called "Rembrandt effects" by nineteenth-century portrait photographers, were used by other painters, as well, notably Henry Inman (see cat. no. 27) and Rembrandt Peale (see cat. no. 30).

Another source of inspiration in Elliott's early career was the art of Gilbert Stuart (see cat. nos. 1-3). Henry T. Tuckerman, one of the first historians of American art, wrote that Elliott owned a Stuart portrait and "from its contemplation he caught the secret of color, the breath and strength of execution which have since placed him among the first American portrait painters." The Stuart portrait was of a Dr. William Hartigan. Painted about 1793, it was later acquired by the noted American collector Thomas B. Clarke and is now in the collection of the National Portrait Gallery in Washington, D. C.

Although he began his artistic career as an itinerant painter in central and western New York State, Charles Loring Elliott had settled in the city of New York by the 1840s. He exhibited his work at the National Academy of Design and became a close friend of Henry Inman, whose own self-portrait (cat. no. 24) is strikingly similar to Elliott's in the use of dramatic lighting and fluid brushwork. After Inman's death in 1846, Elliott became the city's leading portrait painter. During his lifetime, he produced over seven hundred portraits. They ranged in size from bust-length images, such as his self-portrait, to full-length portraits of New York's leading citizens, painted in the grand manner.

References:

Henry T. Tuckerman, *Book of the Artists*, New York: James F. Carr, 1966 (reprint of 1867 ed.), pp. 300-305.

Theodore Bolton, "Charles Loring Elliott: an Account of His Life and Work," *Art Quarterly* 5 (Winter 1942), pp. 58-96.

Ann C. Van Devanter et al., *American Self-Portraits, 1670-1973*, exhib. cat., New York: E. P. Dutton for International Exhibitions Foundation, 1974, no. 28.

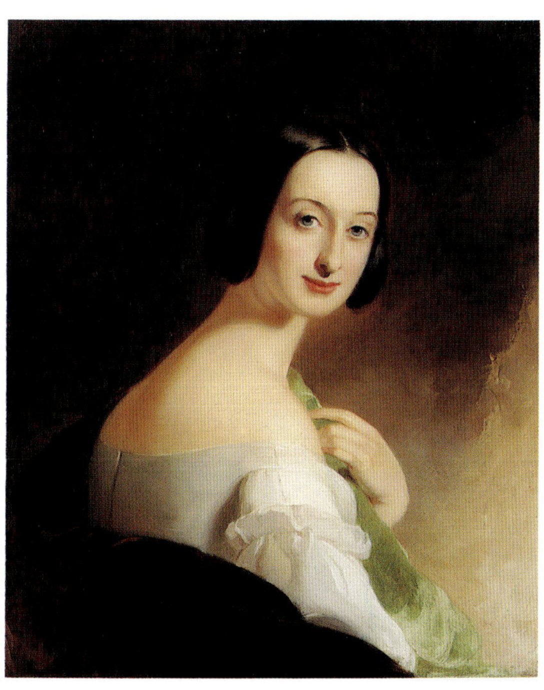

29
Eliza Willing Spring Peters, 1841
Oil on canvas
30 1/8 × 24 13/16 in. (76.5 × 63 cm)
Gift of Mrs. John White Field, 1890.2

According to his account book, Thomas Sully charged a fee of two hundred dollars for this half-length portrait, which was completed in just a few weeks between late January and mid-February, 1841. Like other members of her socially prominent family, Eliza Peters (1820-1902) sought out the most fashionable artist of the day to paint her portrait. Gilbert Stuart had painted a likeness of her mother about 1803, and Rembrandt Peale had painted her grandfather and her father by about 1810. These portraits and a double portrait of Eliza with her husband, John White Field, by John Singer Sargent (cat. no. 38) were among the many works given by the Fields to the Pennsylvania Academy of the Fine Arts.

The Sully portrait of Eliza Peters, painted the year of her marriage, depicts an elegantly dressed young woman with a long, graceful neck and bare shoulders. The softness of Sully's brushwork and the hazy, atmospheric background emphasize the stereotypical feminine qualities of his subject. The painting shows Eliza Peters coiffed in a modish Victorian hairstyle. She continued to wear her hair this way long after it ceased to be fashionable, thus suggesting the conservative nature of her personality.

References:

Edward Biddle and Mantle Fielding, *The Life and Works of Thomas Sully*, Philadelphia: Wickersham Press, 1921, no. 1367.

Catalogue of the Memorial Exhibition of Portraits by Thomas Sully, exhib. cat., Philadelphia: Pennsylvania Academy of the Fine Arts, 1922, no. 2.

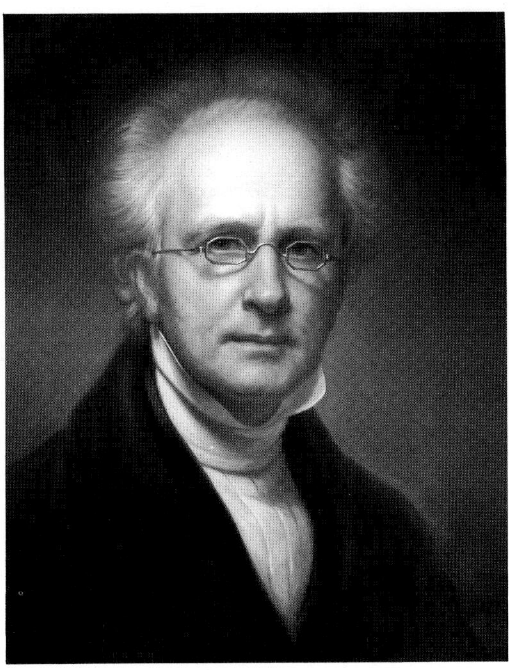

30
Self-Portrait, ca. 1845
Oil on paper, mounted on canvas
$20^3/_4 \times 16^{15}/_{16}$ in. (52.7 × 43 cm)
Bequest of Mrs. Rembrandt Peale, 1869.1

•

Eyeglasses were important to Rembrandt Peale; and, at the age of seventy-nine, he wrote an eloquent appreciation of their significance: "Perhaps there is no recollection of greater value, than my experience in regard to the preservation of sight, which can be duly appreciated by no class of human beings, more than by artists" (*Crayon* 3 [June 1856], p. 163). This self-portrait, completed when he was in his sixties, is related to an earlier one by his father, Charles Willson Peale (cat. no. 6), executed when he was about the same age. Rembrandt Peale's image includes the same bright highlighting of the forehead, emphasis on the glasses, and simple background. The painting well may have been conceived as an homage to his father. The use of paper mounted on canvas also has precedents in his father's work. Charles Willson Peale had used it in a self-portrait (unlocated) that he described to his son when Rembrandt was studying in Paris (letter dated June 26, 1808, American Philosophical Society Library, Philadelphia).

While in Paris, Rembrandt Peale developed his mature style, which differed markedly from that of his father. After two trips to France between 1808 and 1810, Rembrandt adopted a porcelainlike finish and detailed realism in his work. He was influenced by the smooth surfaces and tight execution found in the work of French neoclassical painters, such as Jean-Jacques David, Francois Gerard, and Anne Louis Girodet de Roucy. In this portrait, the large scale of his features and his close proximity to the picture plane give the work an air of immediacy and directness. Such realism became increasingly popular in mid-nineteenth-century portraiture, perhaps as a response to the introduction of photography.

References:

Carol Eaton Hevner and Lillian B. Miller, *Rembrandt Peale, 1778-1860, A Life in the Arts*, exhib. cat., Philadelphia: Historical Society of Pennsylvania, 1985, pp. 12-27, 94.

Lillian B. Miller, ed., *The Selected Papers of Charles Willson Peale and His Family*, New Haven: Yale University Press, 1988, vol. 2, p. 1093.

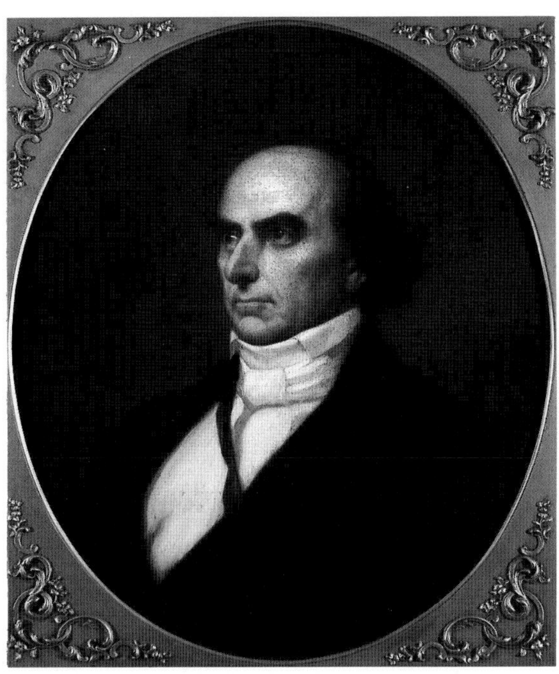

31
Daniel Webster, 1852
Oil on canvas, 30 3/16 × 25 1/8 in. (76.7 × 63.8 cm)
Gift of Mrs. John Frederick Lewis (The John Frederick Lewis Memorial Collection), 1933.10.20

Daniel Webster (1782-1852) was one of nineteenth-century America's most prominent orators. Born in New Hampshire, he was trained as a lawyer in Boston and had a long, distinguished career as a Massachusetts congressman and senator. He also served as secretary of state in the 1840s under two presidents, William Henry Harrison and John Tyler. During this period, George P. A. Healy painted several bust-length portraits of Webster. This one is based on a study made in 1848 (Virginia Museum of Fine Arts, Richmond), which was done in preparation for a large group portrait showing the famous Senate debate between Webster and Robert Y. Hayne over the issue of states' rights (1848-1851, Boston Art Commission, Faneuil Hall). Webster was an ardent Federalist who believed in a strong national government and conservative Whig politics. During the Civil War, stirring phrases from Webster's speeches, such as "Liberty *and* Union, now and forever, one and inseparable," inspired patriotic fervor for the Union cause. Webster had presidential ambitions that he was never able to realize. He pursued an extravagant lifestyle and died of cirrhosis of the liver in 1852. Nevertheless, he was one of the most popular American politicians of the antebellum period. Next to George Washington, he was the political figure most often painted before the Civil War.

Like Webster, Healy began his career in Boston and maintained important connections to that city throughout his career. This portrait, for example, was painted for a Massachusetts congressman, Edward Everett. In the 1830s, Healy went to France to study with Thomas Couture and quickly established an international reputation for portraits of European aristocrats, American politicians, and theatrical celebrities, painted in the grand manner. Webster's important political position and dramatic oratorical style appealed greatly to Healy, who was impressed by the fame of his sitter. Healy's reminiscences are filled with anecdotes about the celebrities that he painted and descriptions of his life among this wealthy, international set.

References:

George P. A. Healy, *Reminiscences of a Portrait Painter*, Chicago: A. C. McClurg and Company, 1894.

Healy's Sitters or A Portrait Panorama of the Victorian Age, exhib. cat., Richmond: Virginia Museum of Art, 1950, p. 23.

James Barber and Frederick Voss, *The Godlike Black Dan, A Selection of Portraits from Life in Commemoration of the Two Hundredth Anniversary of the Birth of Daniel Webster*, exhib. cat., Washington, D. C.: National Portrait Gallery, 1982, pp. 40-43.

1812–1895

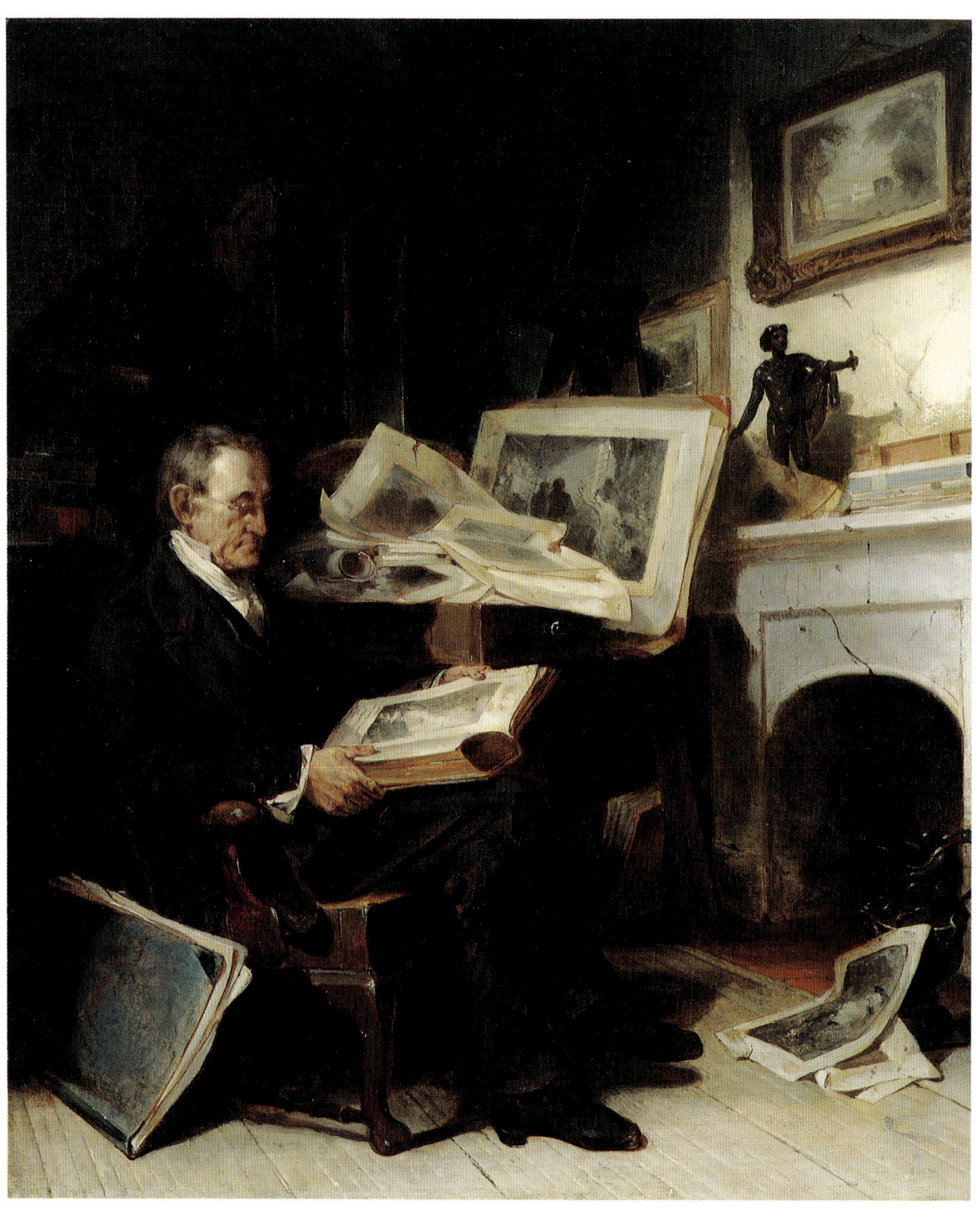

32

The Virtuoso, 1852

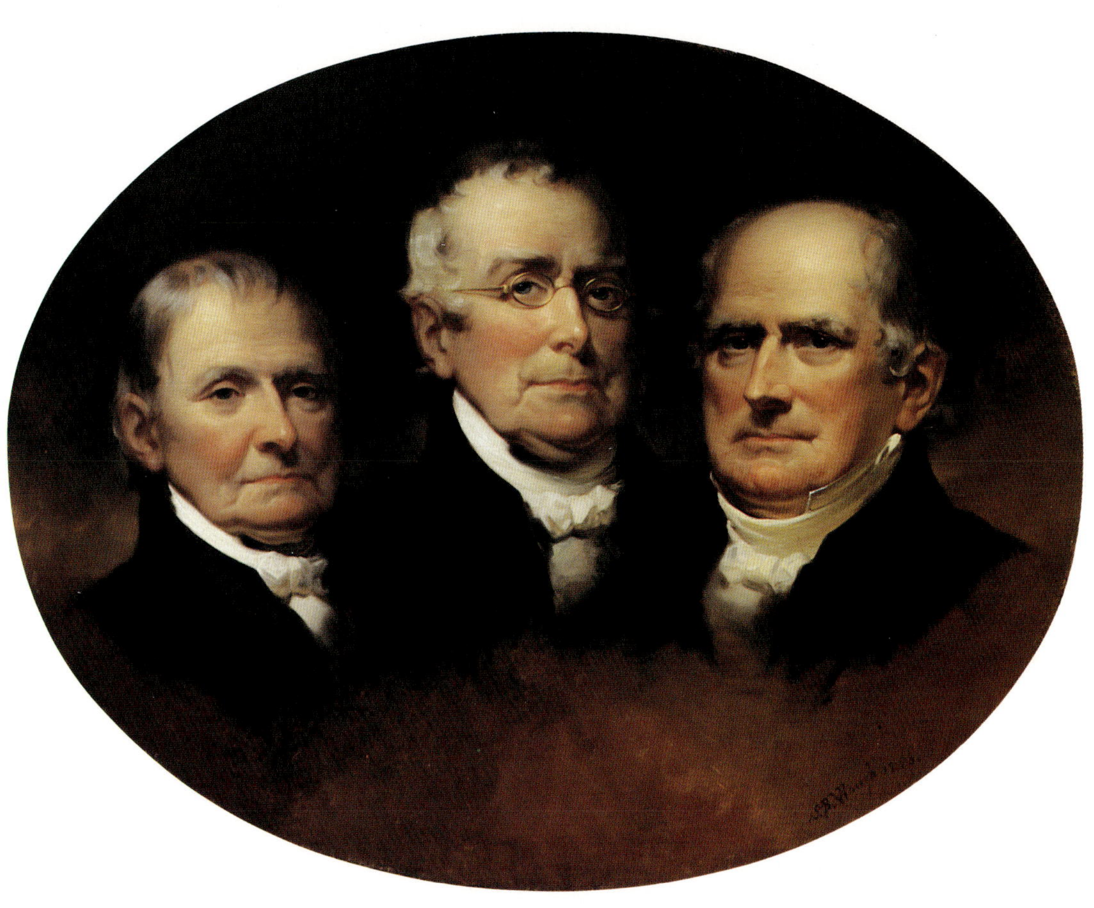

33
Cope Brothers, 1853

1812–1895

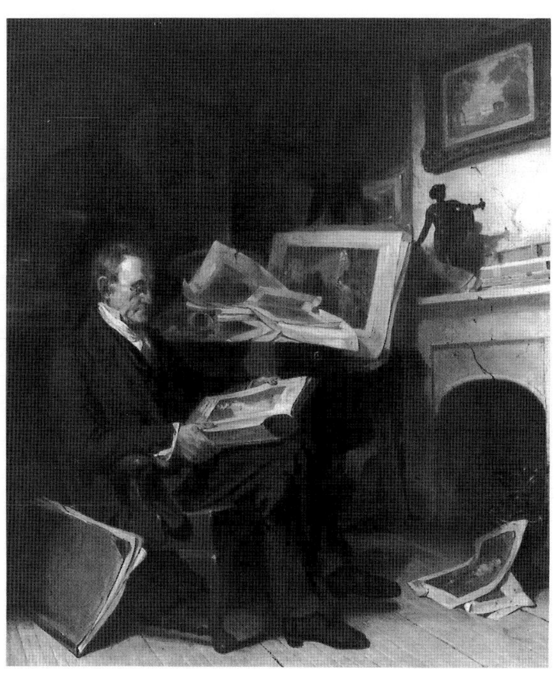

32
The Virtuoso, 1852
Oil on canvas
30 1/2 × 25 1/4 in. (77.5 × 64.1 cm)
Gift of Peter Frederick Rothermel, 1981.12

This may be a portrait of the artist's father-in-law, John Goodhart (dates unknown). Shown here as an art connoisseur, the subject sits in a study cluttered with books, prints, paintings, and sculpture. These details enliven the portrait to such a degree that a contemporary reviewer who saw this work on exhibition at the National Academy of Design in New York noted: "It is an extremely clever little painting. After wandering around the room, we have returned more than once to the old gentleman busied amid his books and portfolios, with the conviction that he is much more of a reality than some of those about him whose names are printed at length in the catalogue. We pray the reader to make his acquaintance" (*Albion* [March 3, 1855], p. 153).

Personalized domestic interiors were commonly used in mid-nineteenth-century portraits (see also cat. no. 34) for the added sense of narrative, or story line, that they give. Rothermel was, in fact, best known as a narrative painter. Although he began his studies in Philadelphia with two portrait painters, John Rubens Smith (1775-1849) and Bass Otis (1784-1861), the major works of his mature career concerned historical subjects. He was one of the most frequent participants in the annual exhibitions of the Pennsylvania Academy of the Fine Arts, where this work was shown in 1853. It was also exhibited at the Paris Salon of 1859 and at the Great Central Fair for the United States Sanitary Commission in Philadelphia in 1864, which helped raise funds for the Union cause during the Civil War.

Reference:

Philadelphia: Three Centuries of American Art, exhib. cat., Philadelphia: Philadelphia Museum of Art, 1976, pp. 371-372.

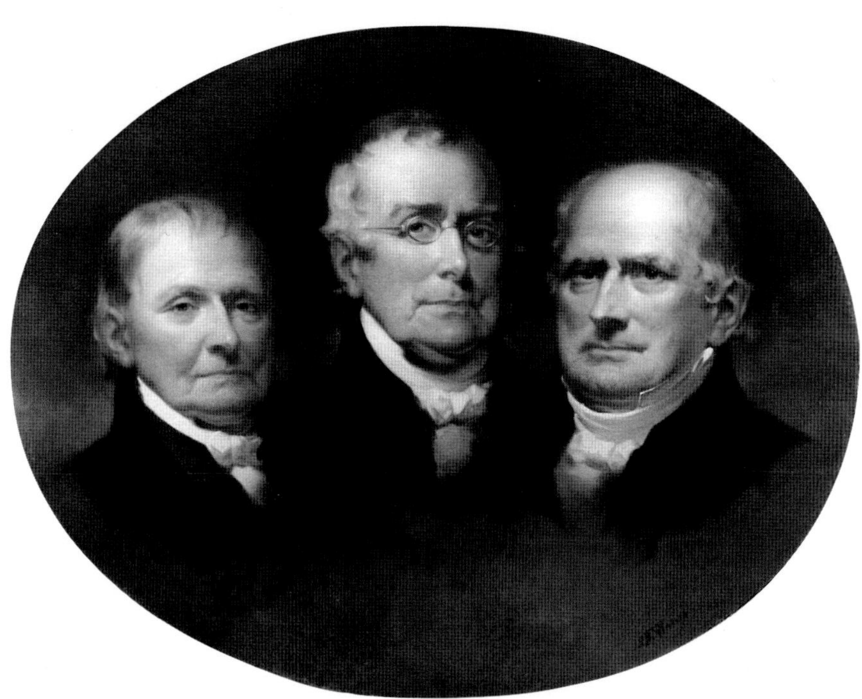

33
Cope Brothers, 1853
Oil on canvas
29 × 35⅝ in. (73.7 × 90.5 cm), oval
Gift of Caleb Cope, 1876.3

The Cope brothers were successful Philadelphia merchants. Thomas Pym Cope (1768-1854), seen at the center of Waugh's portrait, imported dry goods and established the first line of packet ships between Philadelphia and Liverpool in the 1820s. He promoted the completion of the Chesapeake and Delaware Canal and the construction of the Pennsylvania Central Railroad. Members of a prominent Quaker family, Thomas and his brothers, Jasper (left, b. 1775) and Israel (right, b. 1776), were active in philanthropic organizations in Philadelphia. Thomas helped found the Mercantile Library (now the Free Library of Philadelphia), which commissioned John Neagle to paint a portrait of him in 1847. He was also instrumental in acquiring Lemon Hill, an eighteenth-century estate, as a public building for Fairmount Park.

A prolific portrait painter, Samuel Bell Waugh showed his work frequently in the annual exhibitions of the Pennsylvania Academy of the Fine Arts at mid-century. He exhibited a portrait (presently unlocated) of Thomas Pym Cope there in 1851. Group portraits appear to be rare in his work. This painting, with its three bust-length portraits floating in an oval field, is most unusual. Multiple portraits of this form are better known in English art and can be traced to Anthony Van Dyck's *Triple Portrait of Charles I* (ca. 1636, Royal Collection, Windsor Castle).

Caleb Cope, who donated the portrait of the Cope Brothers to the Pennsylvania Academy, was a nephew of the sitters and, at the time of his gift, an active member of the Academy's board of directors.

Reference:

Eliza Cope Harrison, ed., *Philadelphia Merchant, The Diary of Thomas P. Cope*, 1800-1851, South Bend, Ind.: Gateway Editions, 1978.

1823–1859

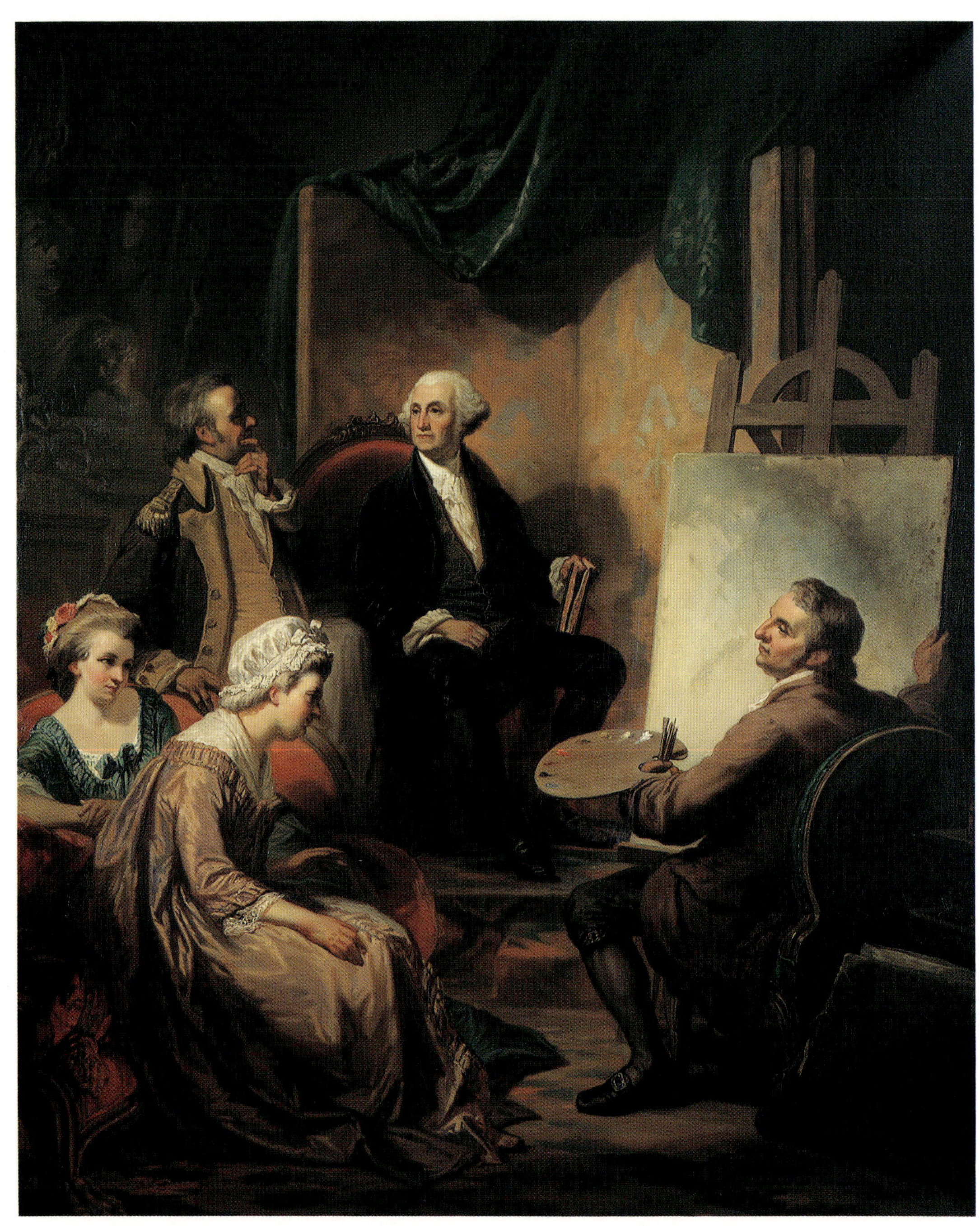

34
Washington Sitting for His Portrait to Gilbert Stuart, 1858

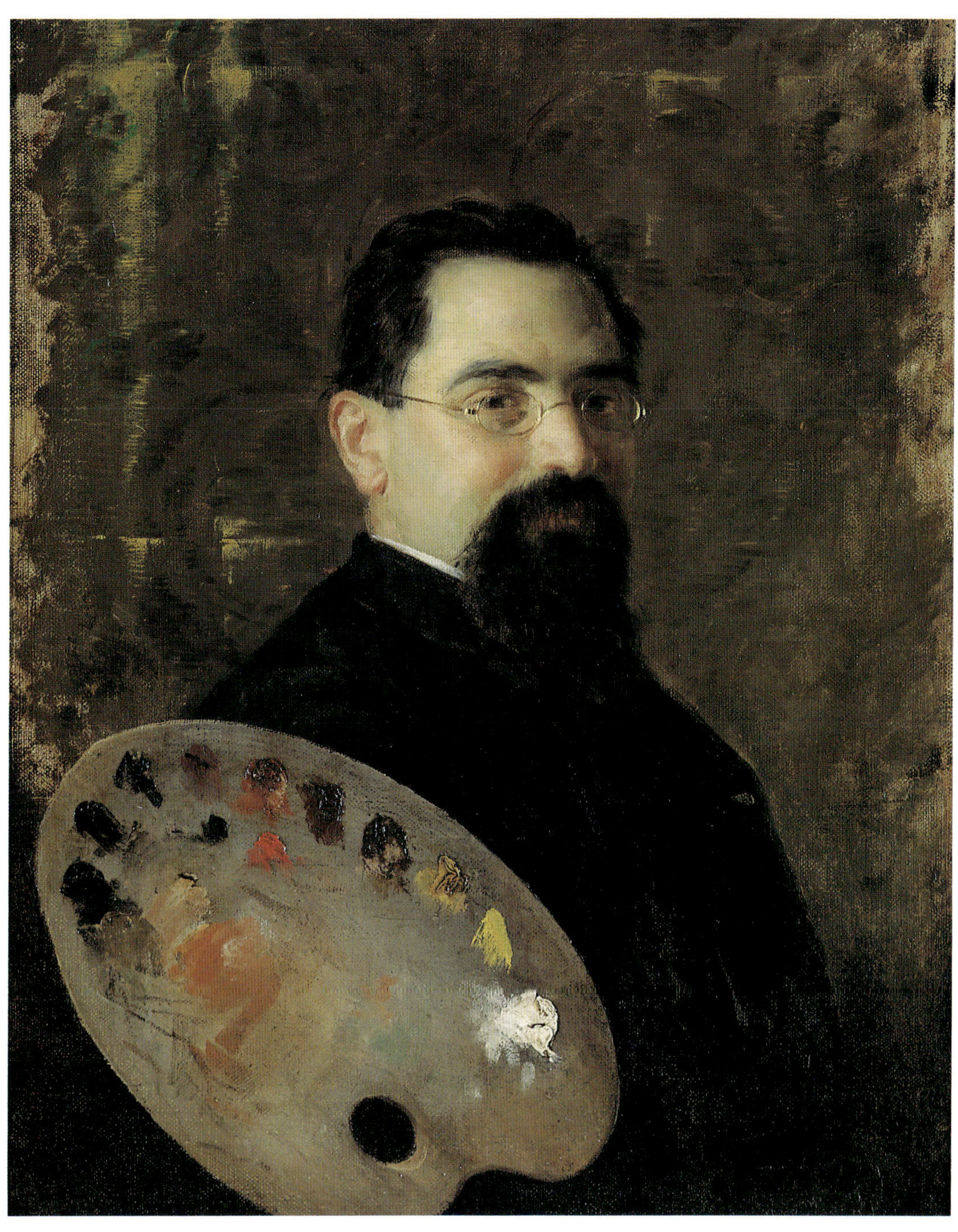

35
Self-Portrait, ca. 1865

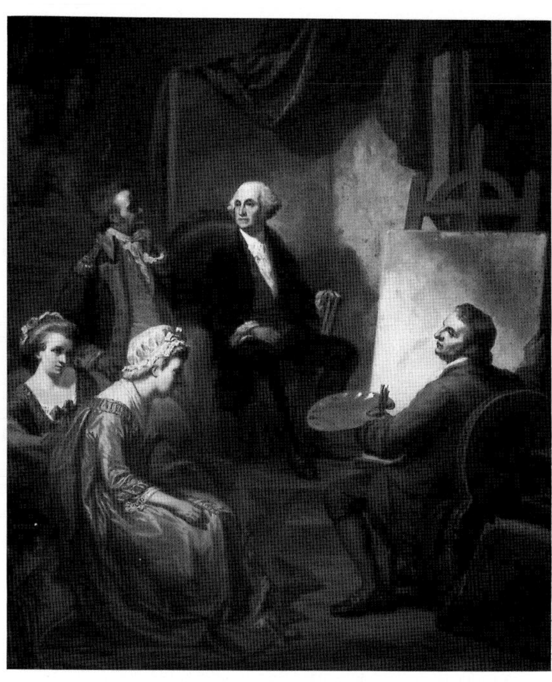

34
WASHINGTON SITTING FOR HIS PORTRAIT TO GILBERT STUART, 1858
Oil on canvas, $50^{3}/_{4} \times 40^{1}/_{2}$ in. (128.9 × 102.9 cm)
Gift of Mrs. John Frederick Lewis (The John Frederick Lewis Memorial Collection), 1933.10.72

This painting, although not strictly a portrait, pays homage to one of America's most celebrated portrait painters. It is a fanciful recreation of the scene in Gilbert Stuart's Germantown studio in 1796 when he painted the famous Athenaeum head of George Washington (cat. no. 1). Martha Washington, who commissioned the Athenaeum head, sits at the left in front of a young woman, probably her daughter, Jane Custis. Washington is seated on a raised dais under a swag of drapery. An unidentified army officer stands at the left. The portrait busts in the background allude not only to classical portraiture but also to the veneration of ancient heroes. In this way, Carl H. Schmolze's painting honors both Washington and the history of portraiture. It further shows that Stuart's Athenaeum head had become a popular icon by the mid-nineteenth century.

Born in Germany, Schmolze took part in the revolutionary activities of that country in the 1840s as a political cartoonist. Forced into exile, he eventually settled in Philadelphia, in 1854. Over the next few years, he exhibited historical subjects and genre scenes at the Pennsylvania Academy of the Fine Arts. This work was shown in the 1858 annual exhibition and was later acquired by John Frederick Lewis for his collection of American portraits.

References:

Mantle Fielding, *Exhibition of American Portraits, Collection of John Frederick Lewis*, exhib. cat., Philadelphia: Pennsylvania Academy of the Fine Arts, 1934, no. 101.

Mark Edward Thistlethwaite, *The Image of George Washington*, New York: Garland Publishing Company, 1979, pp. 4-6.

Richard N. Gregg, *The Artist's Studio in American Painting, 1840-1983*, exhib. cat., Allentown: Allentown Art Museum, 1983, no. 1.

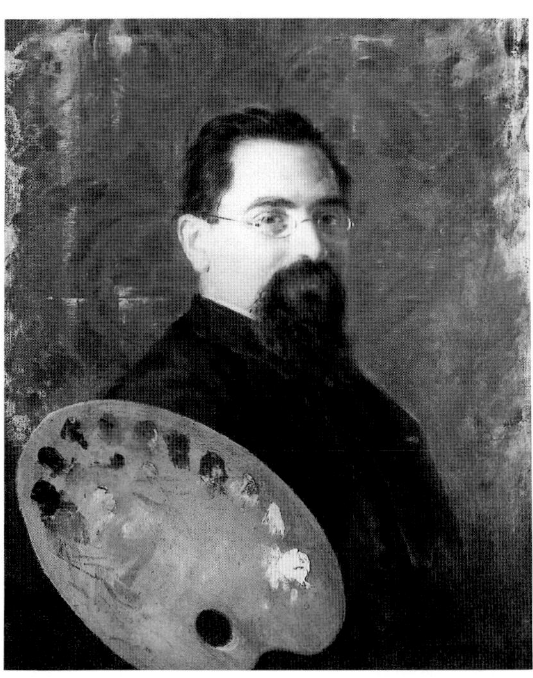

35
Self-Portrait, ca. 1865
Oil on canvas
28⅞ × 23⅝ in. (73.3 × 60 cm)
Gift of John Frederick Lewis, 1928.8.1

•

This unfinished self-portrait not only conveys a notion of Emanuel Leutze's features but also asserts itself as an act of painting. It captures the viewer's attention by the trompe l'oeil depiction of the palette placed conspicuously in the foreground. This device, which also appears in John Neagle's portrait of Thomas Birch (*The Studious Artist*, cat. no. 26), is both a symbol of the artist's occupation and a reminder of the process by which the three-dimensional figure comes alive on the flat canvas.

Leutze, America's leading history painter of the mid-nineteenth century, began his artistic career as a portraitist in Philadelphia. Accounts of the period report that, after the death of his father in 1831, the young Leutze supported his family by drawing portraits for five dollars apiece. By 1834, he was taking art lessons from John Rubens Smith (1775-1849), an English-born artist who encouraged his students to copy portraits from eighteenth-century British prints. The works that Leutze exhibited at the Pennsylvania Academy of the Fine Arts in the early 1840s were predominantly portraits. At the Royal Academy in Düsseldorf in the late 1840s and 1850s, Leutze continued to paint portraits but primarily of family and friends. Among them were likenesses of two fellow students at the Royal Academy: the American artists William Morris Hunt (1824-1879) and Worthington Whittredge (1820-1910). Even after his return to the United States in 1859, when his reputation as a history painter was firmly established, Leutze received portrait commissions from political patrons and well-known literary figures. Nathaniel Hawthorne described in some detail his pleasure at sitting for Leutze—three and a half hours filled with cigars, champagne, and pleasant conversation.

Reference:

Barbara S. Groseclose, *Emanuel Leutze, 1816-1868: Freedom is the Only King*, exhib. cat., Washington, D. C.: National Collection of Fine Arts, Smithsonian Institution, 1975, pp. 13-67.

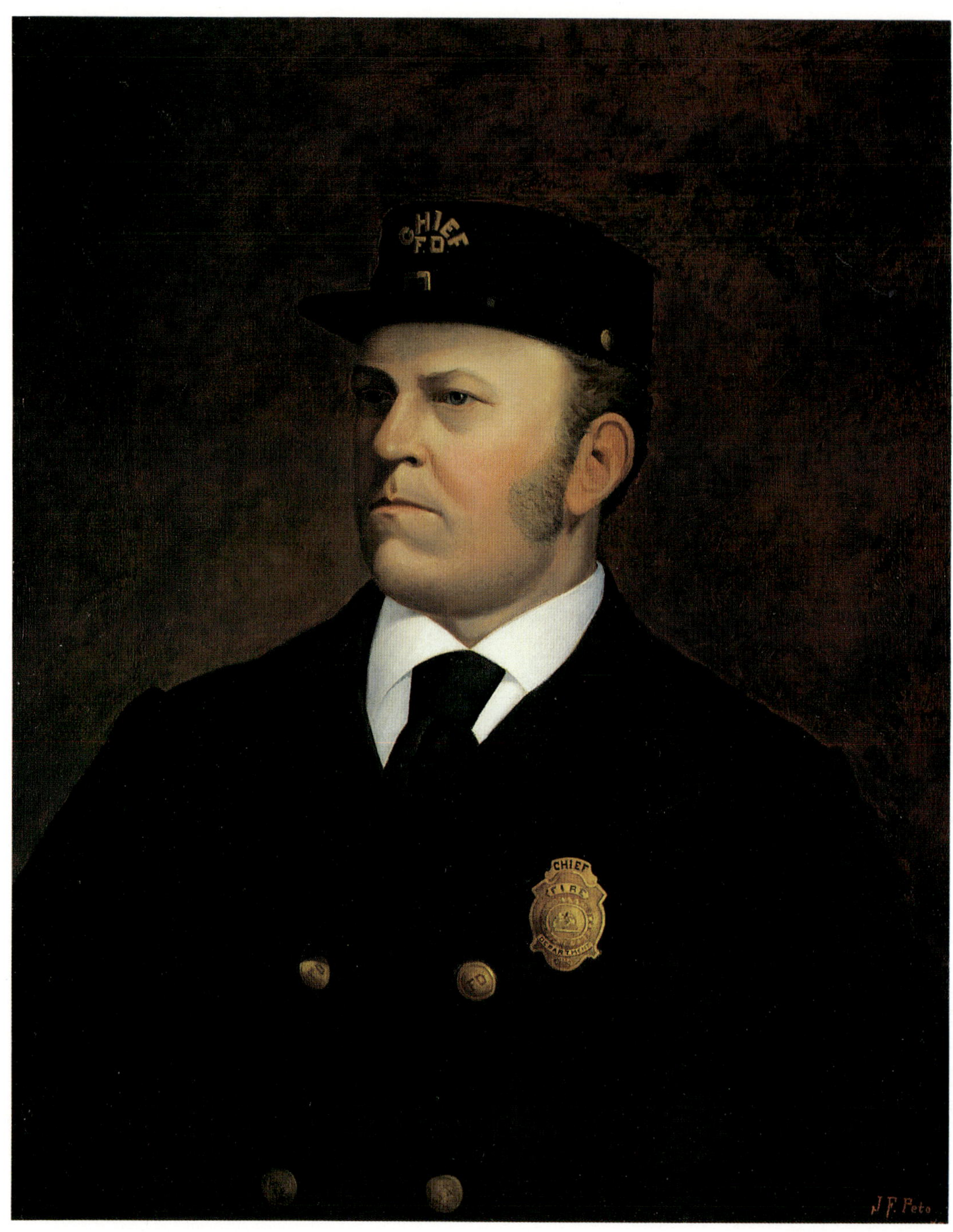

36
The First Fire Chief of Philadelphia:
Portrait of the Artist's Father, 1878

James R. Lambdin
1807–1889

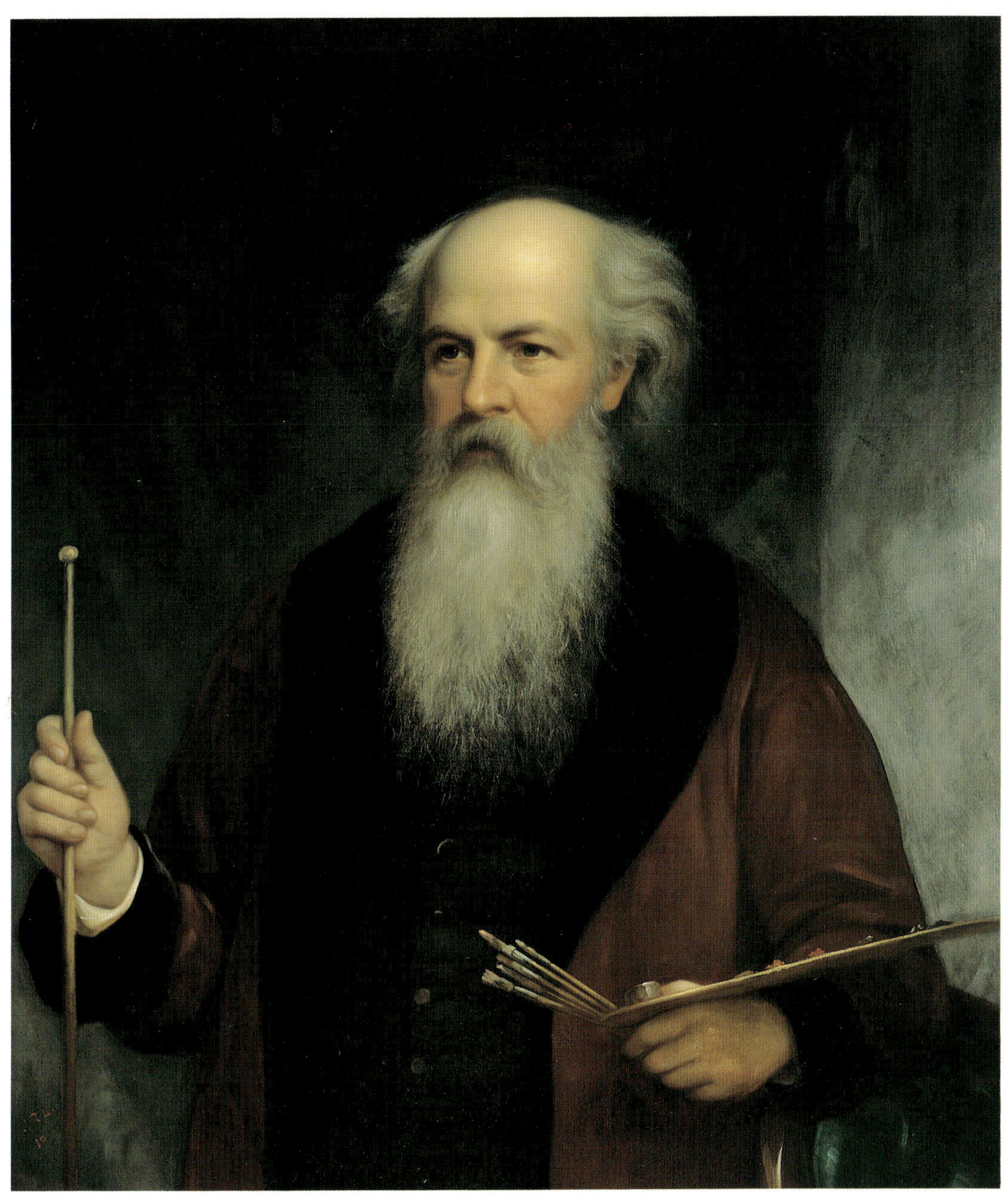

37
Self-Portrait, ca. 1880

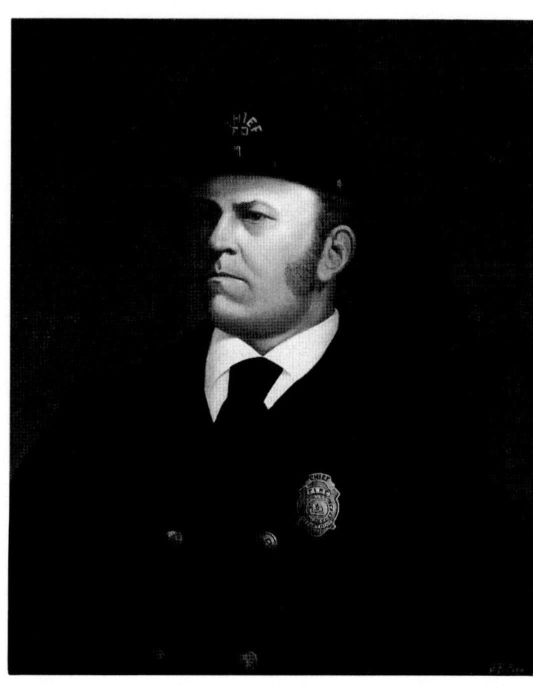

36
The First Fire Chief of Philadelphia: Portrait of the Artist's Father, 1878
Oil on canvas, 31 1/4 × 25 3/16 in. (79.4 × 64 cm)
Gift of the Barra Foundation, 1983.13

•

The sitter, Thomas Hope Peto (1829-1896), sold fire-fighting supplies and was an honorary member of the Philadelphia Fire Department. Although he was not in fact the city's first chief, Peto was the chief marshal of the Hope Hose Company, one of the many volunteer fire companies that existed in Philadelphia during the nineteenth century. These fire companies not only were concerned with public safety but also served as social clubs. Thomas Peto was an avid musician and led the company's marching band. He imparted both his love of music and his fondness for the fire company to his son, John Frederick Peto, who used his father's fire department memorabilia and musical instruments in several of his still-life paintings.

Although known as a still-life painter, John F. Peto began his artistic career as a portrait photographer. His aunt was married to the Philadelphia photographer William Bell (1830-1910); and, at the time this painting was executed, in the late 1870s Peto set up his own photographic studio on Chestnut Street, just a few blocks from Bell. Thomas Peto's stern expression and the crisply rendered details of his clothing in this portrait suggest parallels with the commercial portrait photography of the period. Despite the subject's air of rigid authority, the artist seems to have been genuinely fond of his father from whom he was separated at an early age, when after his mother's death, he was sent to live with his maternal grandmother. As this portrait illustrates, Peto's conception of his father was closely tied to the latter's association with fire fighting. In 1894, two years before his death, Thomas Peto wrote a note asking his son to paint a picture of a fire engine on the front of his ceremonial fire hat. As a memorial, in 1904, the artist painted a trompe l'oeil tombstone that resembled one of his father's business signs.

References:

Alfred Frankenstein, *After the Hunt: William Harnett and Other American Still Life Painters*, 1870-1900, Berkeley and Los Angeles: University of California Press, 1969, p. 99.

John Wilmerding, *Important Information Inside, The Art of John F. Peto and the Idea of Still-Life Painting in Nineteenth-Century America*, exhib. cat., Washington, D. C.: National Gallery of Art, pp. 12-14.

1807–1889

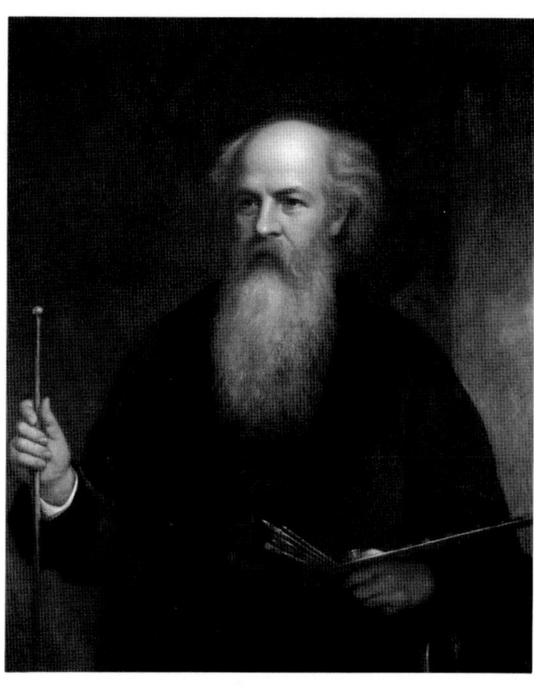

37
Self-Portrait, ca. 1880
Oil on canvas
42 1/2 × 34 in. (108 × 86.4 cm)
Gift of Dr. Alfred C. Lambdin on behalf of the artist's family, 1891.8

James Reid Lambdin was a well-known Philadelphia portrait painter who played an active role in the history of the Pennsylvania Academy of the Fine Arts in the mid-nineteenth century. He was born in Pittsburgh and received his early training from an itinerant portrait painter, or limner. The young boy was much impressed by a copy of Gilbert Stuart's famous portrait of George Washington (see cat. no. 1) made by the limner to serve as a sign over the door of a local coffeehouse. Between 1823 and 1826, Lambdin studied painting in Philadelphia with Thomas Sully (see cat. nos. 12, 16, and 29). At that time, Lambdin must have visited Charles Willson Peale's museum, because, on his return to Pittsburgh in 1828, Lambdin set up the first museum there. Like Peale's, it contained both works of art and specimens of natural history. In addition to landscape paintings by contemporary artists, such as Thomas Doughty (1793-1856) and Thomas Birch (1779-1851), Lambdin exhibited his own work and portraits by Stuart (see cat. nos. 1-3), Sully, and Peale (see cat. no. 6).

In the 1830s, Lambdin began to travel beyond Pittsburgh to the southern states in search of portrait commissions. He finally settled in Philadelphia in 1837 and remained there for the rest of his life. Lambdin became a frequent participant in the annual exhibitions at the Pennsylvania Academy of the Fine Arts. He also served on the board of directors and was chairman of the committees on finance and instruction. A prominent portraitist, he painted likenesses of the fifteen United States presidents from John Quincy Adams to James A. Garfield. In this self-portrait, Lambdin depicts himself as a rather patriarchal figure with a long beard. He holds the tools of his trade—a maulstick, a palette, and brushes. The strong highlight on his high forehead suggests the influence of self-portraits by members of the Peale family, especially Charles Willson Peale's *The Artist in His Museum* (fig. 1).

References:

John O'Connor, Jr., "Reviving a Forgotten Artist, a sketch of James Reid Lambdin—The Pittsburgh Painter of American Statesmen," *Carnegie Magazine* 12 (Sept. 1938), pp. 115-118.

Southwestern Pennsylvania Painters, 1800-1945, exhib. cat., Greensburg, Pa.: Westmoreland County Museum of Art, 1981, no. 150.

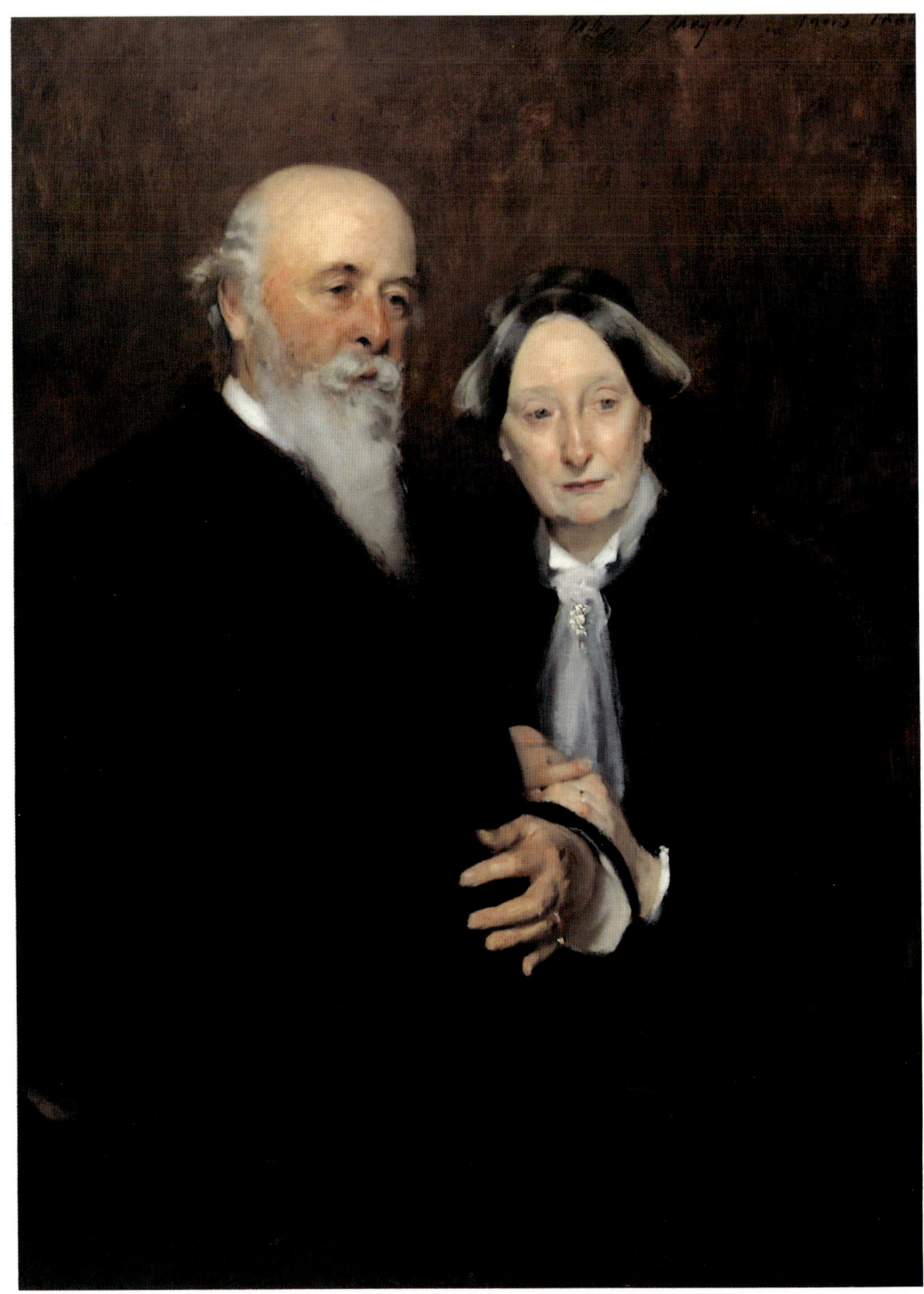

38
Mr. and Mrs. John White Field, 1882

1855–1942

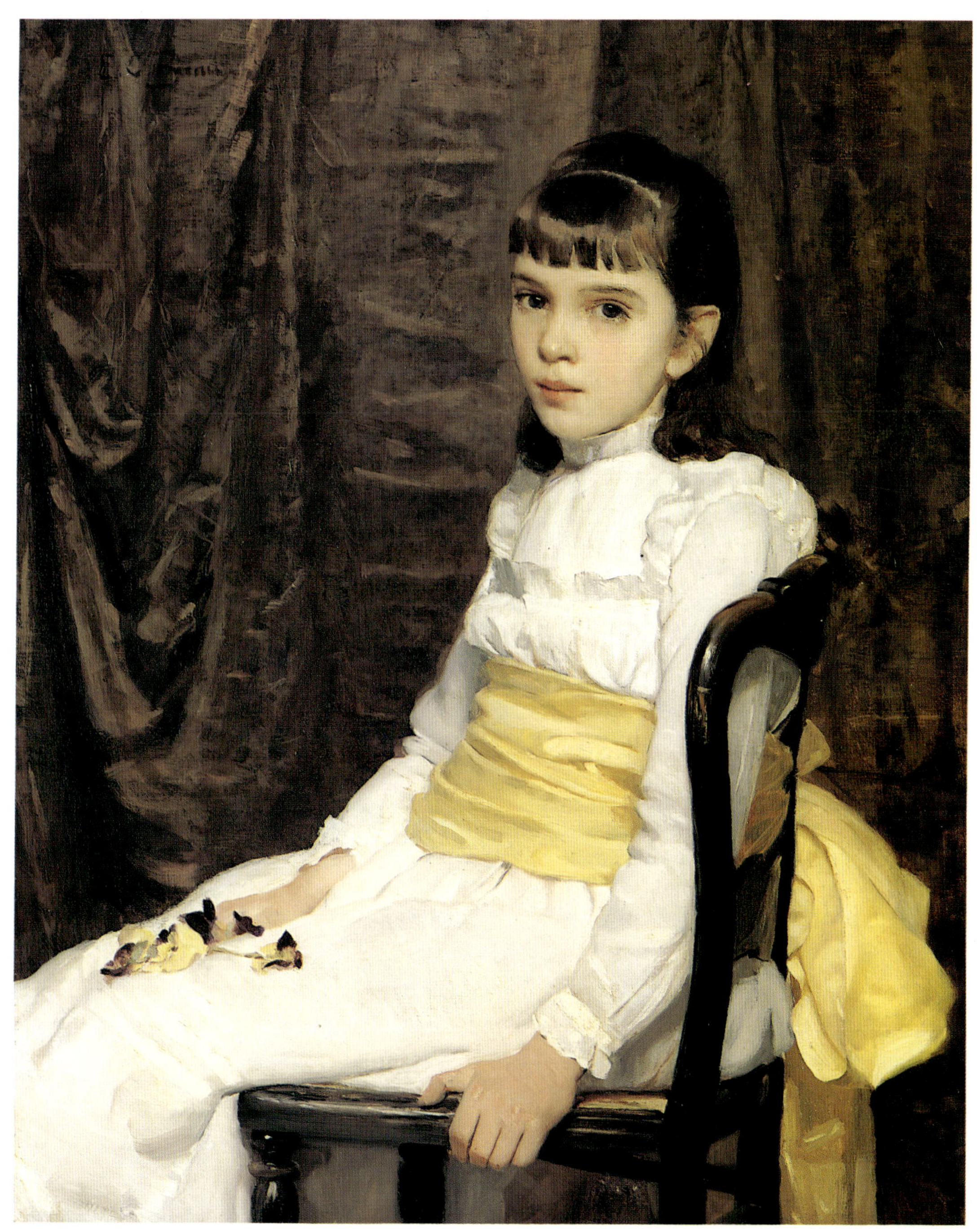

39
A Little Girl, 1887

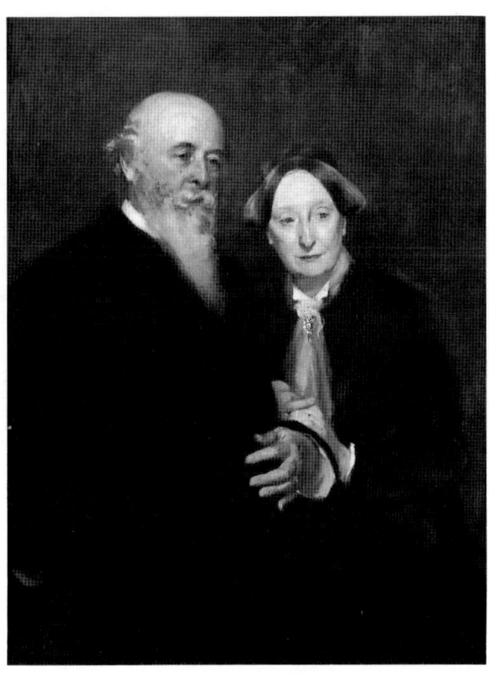

38
Mr. and Mrs. John White Field, 1882
Oil on canvas
44 7/8 × 32 in. (114 × 81.3 cm)
Gift of Mr. and Mrs. John White Field, 1891.10

John White Field (1815-1887) and his wife, Eliza Peters Field (1820-1902), were wealthy members of an international social set that included some of the most noted writers and artists of the late nineteenth century. Among their acquaintances were literary figures such as Robert Browning, Charles Eliot Norton, and James Russell Lowell and the sculptor William Wetmore Story (1819-1895). The couple married in 1841 and over the years lived in Newport, Washington, London, and Paris—as well as Philadelphia. They were avid art collectors and acquired works by both European and American artists, many of which were given to the Pennsylvania Academy of the Fine Arts.

As the leading expatriate portrait painter of his day, John Singer Sargent had a reputation for depicting the elegance and aloofness of the upper class. In this portrait, however, he concentrated on the personal relationship between his sitters rather than the social trappings of their class. When this work was shown in a 1924 exhibition of Sargent's work, a critic praised it as a masterful interpretation of old age. The reviewer noted how convincingly Sargent had captured the nature of the Fields's long marriage in their clasped hands and the subtle inclination of their heads toward one another. She also observed a suggestion of deference in Mrs. Field's pose and a "considerate and gentle" expression of protectiveness on the part of her husband. Sargent's ability to convey the nuances of age in facial expression alone are even more evident when this portrait is compared to Thomas Sully's image of the youthful Mrs. Field, painted the year that she was married (cat. no. 29).

References:

Rose V. S. Berry, "John Singer Sargent: Some of His American Work," *Art and Archeology* 18 (Sept. 1924), p. 103.

Patricia Hills et al., *John Singer Sargent*, exhib. cat., New York: Whitney Museum of American Art, 1987, no. 107.

1855–1942

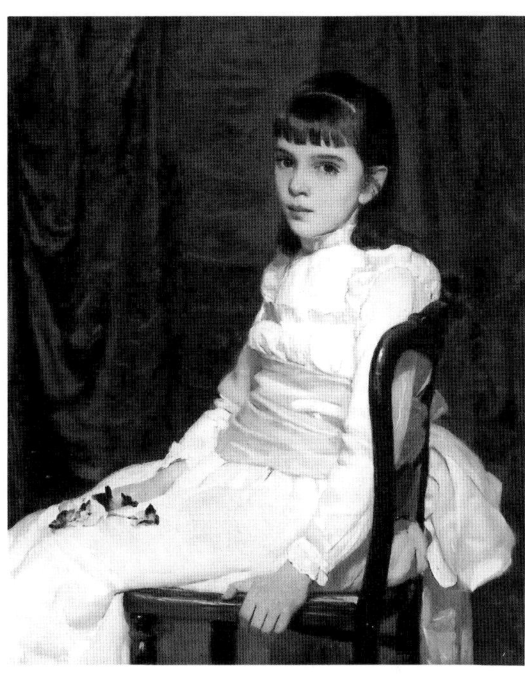

39
A Little Girl, 1887
Oil on canvas
36 × 29 3/16 in. (91.4 × 74.1 cm)
Gift of Fanny Travis Cochran, 1955.12

Depicted here as a quiet and demure ten-year-old, Fanny Travis Cochran (1876-1977) grew up to become a militant social activist. As the daughter of Travis Cochran, a prominent Philadelphia wine merchant, she enjoyed the privileges of wealth and social status that were common at the turn of the century: summers sailing the family yacht off Campobello Island, Maine; a grand tour of Europe; and an education at Bryn Mawr College, from which she was graduated in 1904. By 1910, she had become involved in the movement to improve working conditions in Pennsylvania factories. She and a Quaker activist friend, Florence L. Sanville, worked in a Scranton silk mill to experience sweatshop conditions firsthand so that they could better lobby for reforms. That same year, Cochran was arrested for participating in a shirt-factory strike in Philadelphia. She used her inheritance to establish a home for working girls, and she volunteered much of her time to teach English in local prisons and settlement houses. Even at the age of one hundred, she still read books written by women about social change, such as Harriet Beecher Stowe's *Uncle Tom's Cabin* and Jane Austen's *Pride and Prejudice*.

Like Cochran, the artist came from a privileged Philadelphia family and fought hard to lead an independent life as a woman. After studying at the Pennsylvania Academy of the Fine Arts and abroad, Cecilia Beaux became one of Philadelphia's leading portrait painters in the late nineteenth century. Her earliest portraits, with their limited range of color, asymmetrical placement of chairs, and simple backgrounds, reflect the influence of James Abbott McNeill Whistler (1834-1903). His famous portrait *Arrangement in Gray and Black, No. 1: The Artist's Mother* (1871/72, Musée du Louvre, Paris) was exhibited at the Pennsylvania Academy in 1881, when Beaux was a student there. She later became an instructor at the Academy, where she taught portraiture from 1895 to 1916.

References:

Cecilia Beaux: Portrait of an Artist, exhib. cat., Philadelphia: Pennsylvania Academy of the Fine Arts, 1974, no. 24.

Judith E. Stein, "Profile of Cecilia Beaux," *Feminist Art Journal* 4 (Winter 1975/76), pp. 25-31.

Tara Tappert, "Choices—The Life and Career of Cecilia Beaux: A Professional Biography," Ph.D. diss., George Washington University, 1990, pp. 303-316.

"Fanny T. Cochran; Crusader was one hundred," *Philadelphia Inquirer*, June 18, 1977, p. 21.

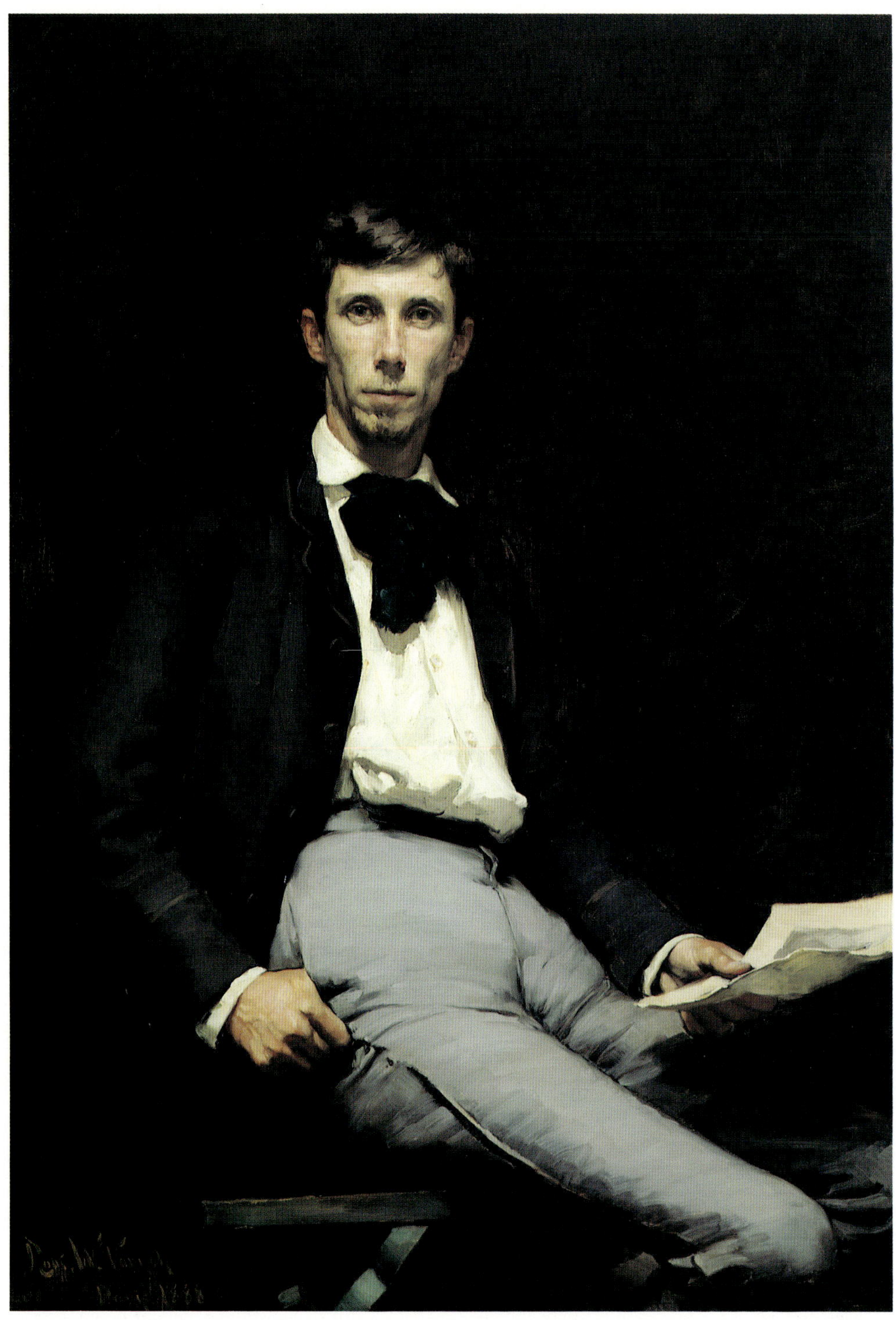

40
Companion of the Studio, 1888

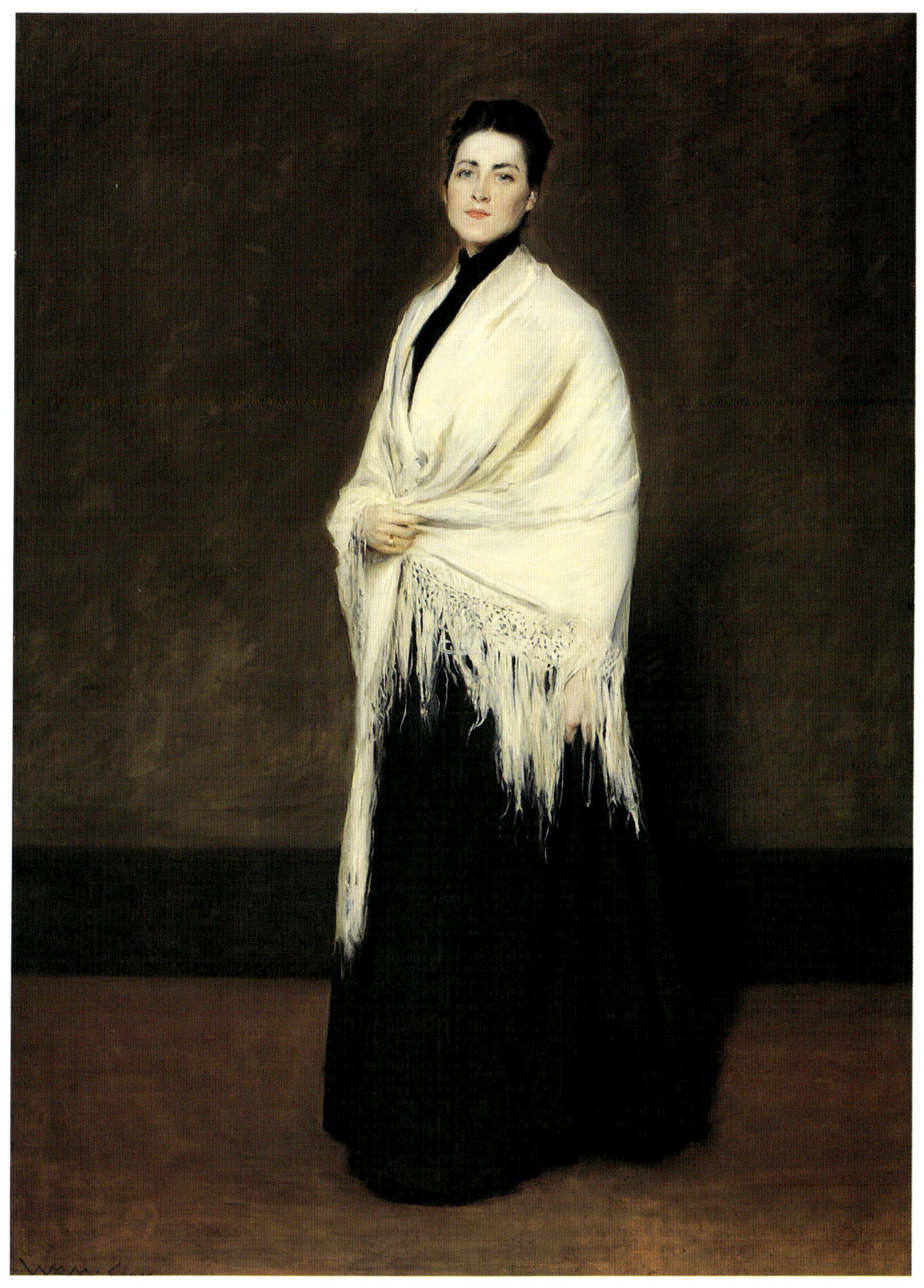

41
Portrait of Mrs C. (Lady with a White Shawl), 1893

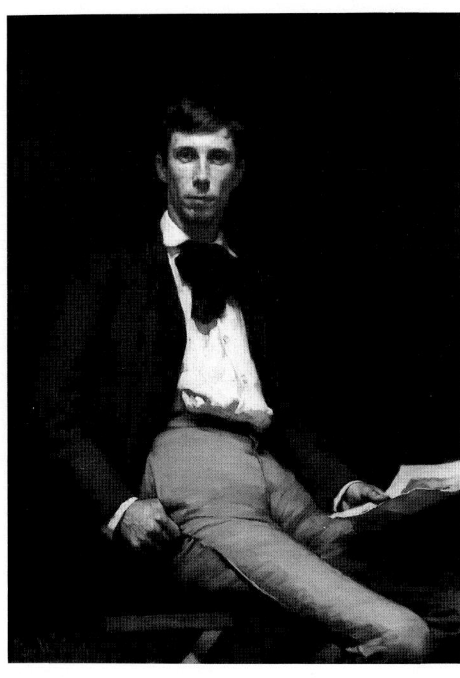

40
COMPANION OF THE STUDIO, 1888
Oil on canvas
51¹/₄ × 36¹/₄ in. (130.2 × 92.1 cm)
Joseph E. Temple Fund, 1891.14

Robert W. Vonnoh was a successful Boston portraitist, who, like many of his fellow painters in the late nineteenth century, also worked abroad. This portrait was executed during his second trip to France, when his style was in a period of transition from somber realism to a more impressionistic manner. Although he spent a great deal of time painting landscapes during his stay from 1886 to 1891, it was this portrait that he chose to exhibit at the prestigious 1889 Universal Exposition in Paris, where he won a bronze medal.

The subject was a fellow student at the Académie Julian in Paris—John Charles Pinhey (1860-1912), a Canadian portraitist who occasionally produced landscapes and figure studies. Probably executed early in 1888, this work displays the academic method of painting espoused by the more conservative art schools of the period. Although the individual brushstrokes that model the figure are visible at close range, they merge at a distance to suggest solid, three-dimensional form. The dark tonalities in the clothing and the serious expression and direct gaze of the sitter are stylistic features shared with the work of Cecilia Beaux (see cat. no. 39) and William Merritt Chase (see cat. no. 41), who, like Vonnoh, taught portraiture at the Pennsylvania Academy of the Fine Arts in the 1890s. *Companion of the Studio* was shown in the 1891 annual exhibition at the Pennsylvania Academy and was purchased for the permanent collection that year.

References:

May Brawley Hill, *Grez Days: Robert Vonnoh in France*, exhib. cat., New York: Berry-Hill Galleries, 1987, p. 16.

Annette Blaugrund et al., *Paris 1889, American Artists at the Universal Exposition*, exhib. cat., Philadelphia: Pennsylvania Academy of the Fine Arts, 1989, pp. 222-223.

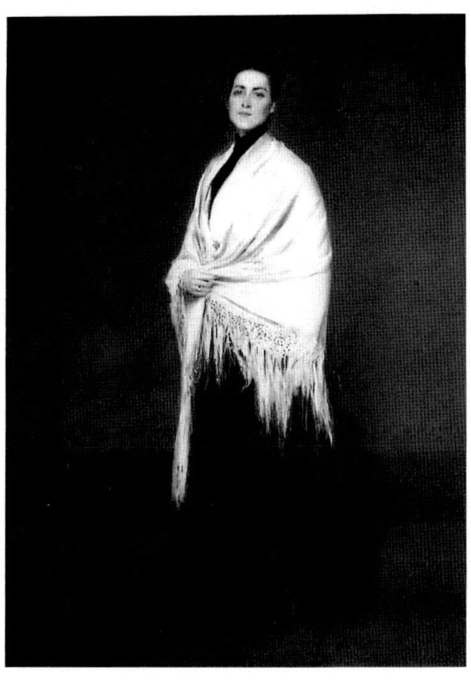

41
Portrait of Mrs. C. (Lady with a White Shawl), 1893
Oil on canvas
75 × 52 in. (190.5 × 132.1 cm)
Joseph E. Temple Fund, 1895.1

There has been much speculation about the identity of the subject of this portrait, whom Chase described as "the perfect type of American womanhood." It has been suggested that she was Chase's wife or perhaps Emily Jewell Clark, a wealthy art collector from Michigan. Her features do not resemble those of Mrs. Chase, however, and Mrs. Clark would have been fifty at the time of this painting, certainly too old to be the fashionable young woman depicted here. The same unnamed woman appears in several of Chase's other undated paintings of the period: *The Opera Cloak* (Grand Rapids Museum of Art), *Portrait of a Lady in White* (collection of Mr. and Mrs. Meredith Long, Houston), and *A Lady in Evening Dress* (Museum of Fine Arts, Boston). One of the artist's favorite models at the time that these portraits were painted was Minnie Clark, who also posed for the popular magazine illustrator Charles Dana Gibson (1867-1944). Gibson used her features in creating his famous "Gibson Girl," the epitome of the modern American woman at the turn of the century. Chase's use of only the subject's initial and a generic title for the Pennsylvania Academy's painting suggests a similar tendency to conceive of his portrait as an ideal type.

Portrait of Mrs. C. was one of sixteen works by Chase shown in the annual exhibition of 1894 at the Pennsylvania Academy of the Fine Arts. It was chosen to be illustrated in the catalogue. The portrait was also shown abroad in Paris (1899 and 1900) and Berlin (1908). In such exhibitions, Chase's work was often hung next to the society portraits of John Singer Sargent (see cat. no. 38) because both artists were adept at suggesting the suavity and aloofness of the upper class with their elegant costumes and haughty poses. This kind of portraiture dominated both the exhibitions and the studios of the Pennsylvania Academy, where Chase taught between 1896 and 1909.

References:

Ronald G. Pisano, *William Merritt Chase*, New York: Watson-Guptill Publications, 1979, p. 66, pl. 24.

Carolyn Kinder Carr, *William Merritt Chase: Portraits*, exhib. cat., Akron: Akron Art Museum, 1982, pp. 19-21.

1855–1941

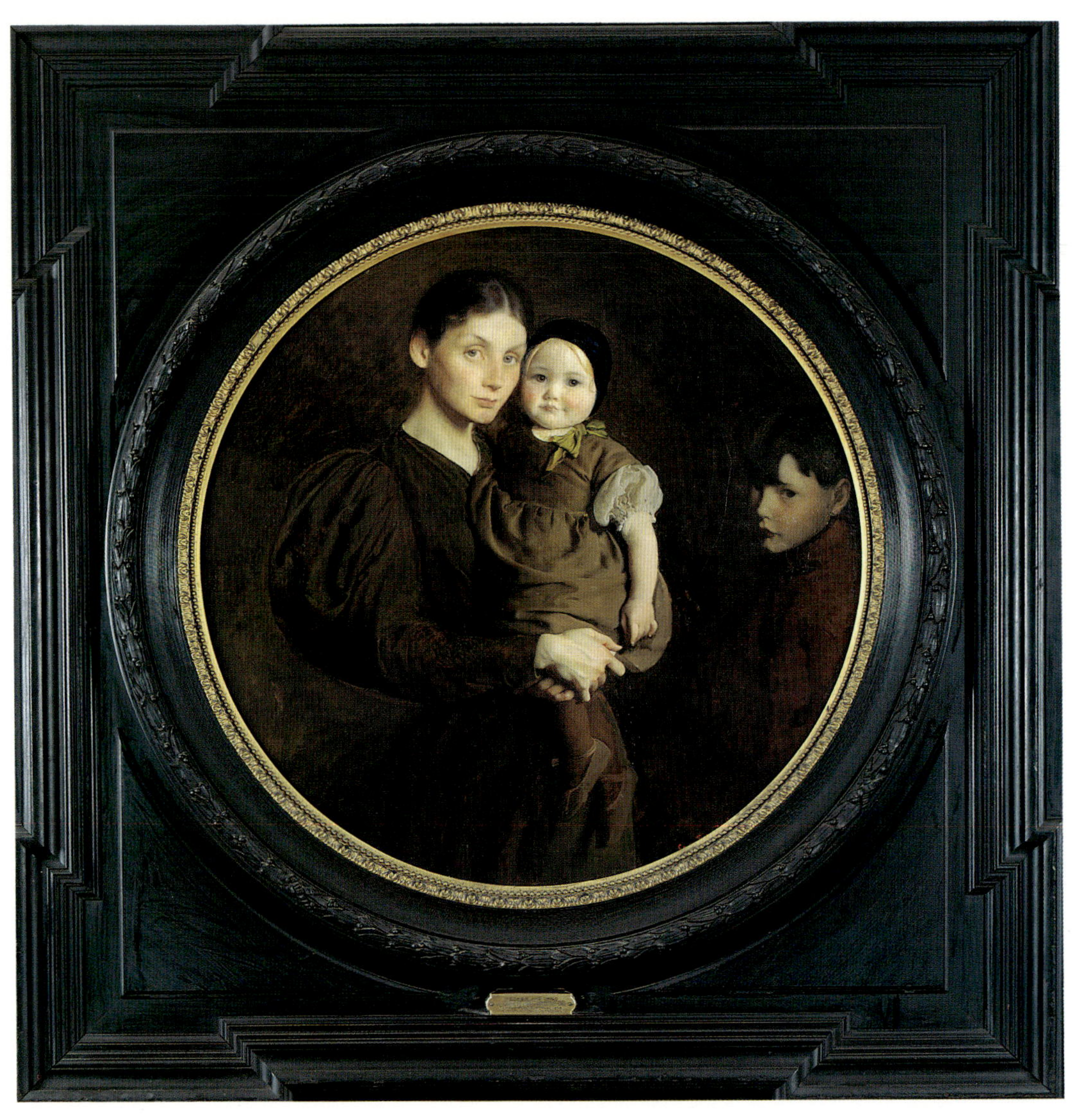

42

Mother and Child, ca. 1897

1844–1916

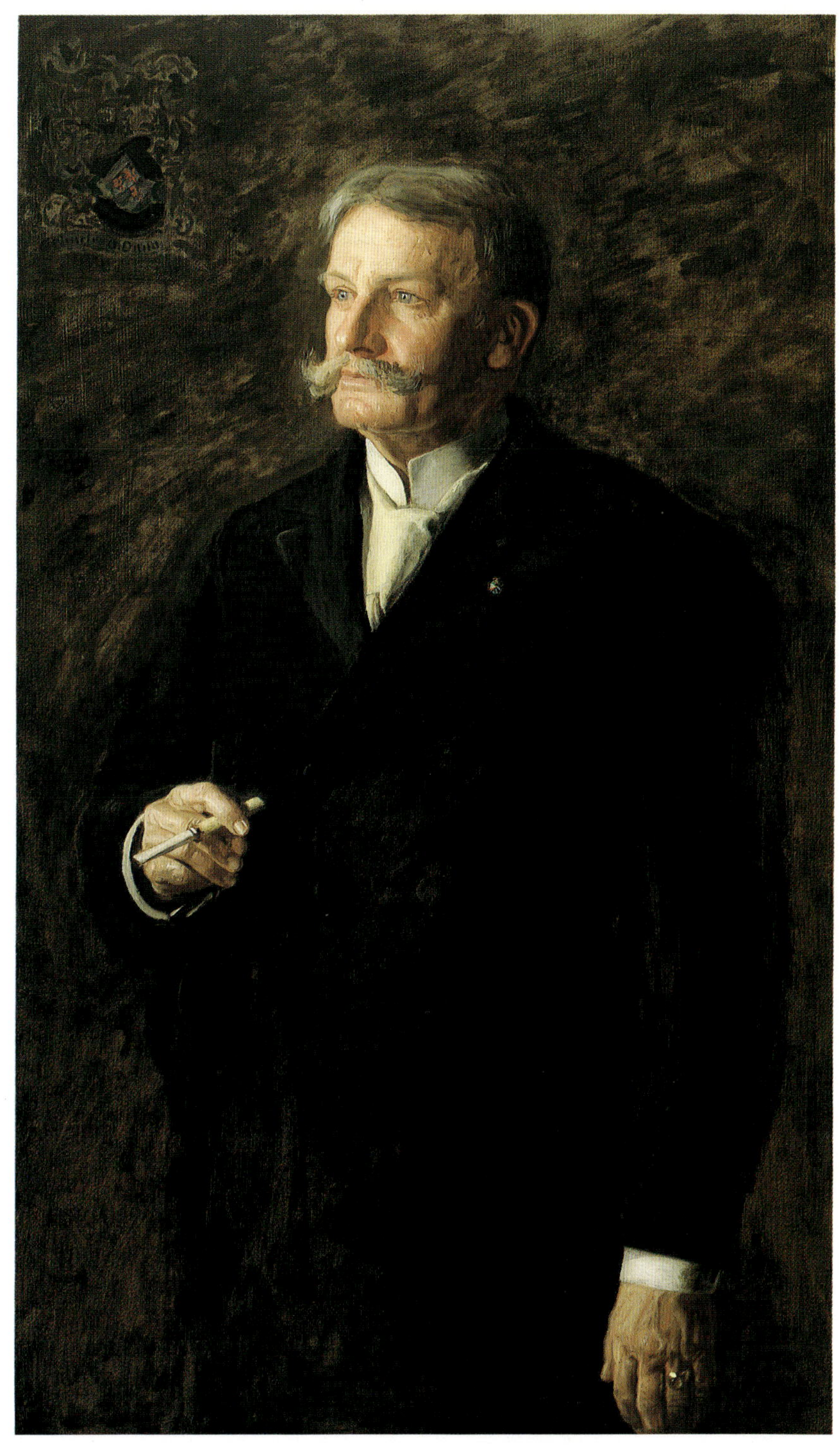

43
Charles Edmund Dana, ca. 1902

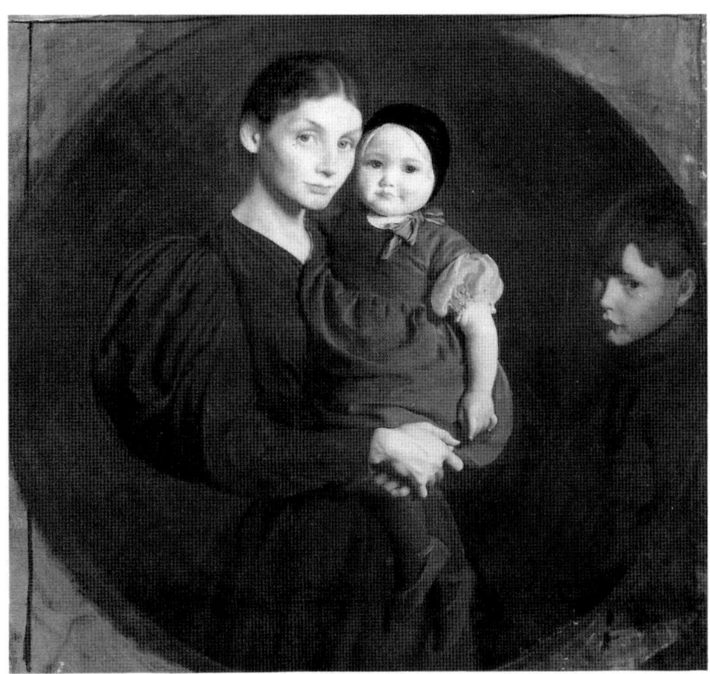

42
Mother and Child, ca. 1897
Oil on canvas
39¼ in. dia. (99.7 cm)
Joseph E. Temple Fund, 1898.2

Active in the American Renaissance movement, George de Forest Brush is best known for portraits of his family that evoke images of the Madonna and Christ Child. The dozen or so paintings of his wife and children executed in the 1890s established his reputation. Art critics of his day frequently pointed out that Brush's paintings were not mere imitations of Italian religious art but realistic portraits that appealed to contemporary American audiences. Brush was praised for introducing "a modern note of painful seriousness" and avoiding sentimentality. His family portraits were viewed as forthright representations of maternal responsibility that expressed universal truths.

This portrait of the artist's wife, Mittie (ca. 1866-1949), with two of their children, Gerome (b. 1888) and probably Georgia (b. 1895), is presented in a tondo, or round format, that further emphasizes the relationship of the image to Italian Renaissance art. Painters such as Raphael and Andrea del Sarto frequently used this format in their images of the Virgin and Child and often included the figure of Saint John standing to one side. The frame on Brush's portrait, which is original to the work, imitates a seventeenth-century Dutch style frame. This suggests another pictorial source used by the artist in his adaptation of European precedents. The portrait's limited range of color, the simple background, and the realistic depiction of facial features link Brush's work not only to Dutch art but also to such popular late nineteenth-century American portrait painters as William Merritt Chase (see cat. no. 41) and Thomas Eakins (see cat. no. 43). Their work was often featured in the annual exhibitions at the Pennsylvania Academy of the Fine Arts, where this painting was awarded a Temple Gold Medal in 1897. It was purchased the following year for the Academy's permanent collection.

References:

Charles Caffin, *The Story of American Painting*, New York: Fred Stokes and Co., 1907, pp. 180-181.

Joan B. Morgan, *George de Forest Brush, 1855-1941, Master of the American Renaissance*, exhib. cat., New York: Berry-Hill Galleries, 1985, no. 32, pp. 23-28.

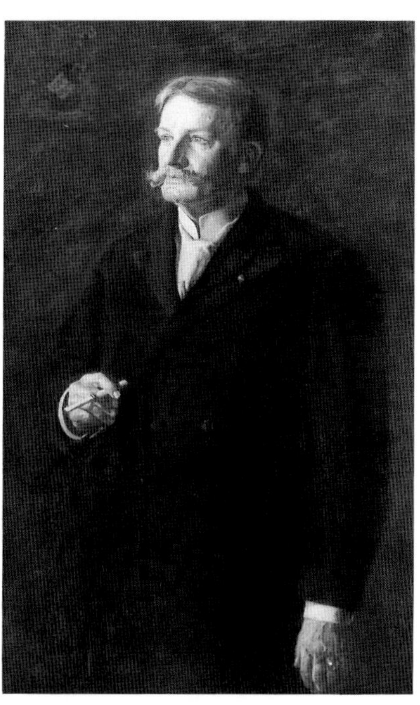

43
Charles Edmund Dana, ca. 1902
Oil on canvas
50¹/₄ × 30¹/₈ in. (127.6 × 76.5 cm)
Gift of Charles Edmund Dana, 1913.16

Charles Edmund Dana (1843-1914) was an artist, teacher, and author who was active in Philadelphia art circles at the turn of the century. Like Eliza Peters Field (cat. no. 38), Dana was a descendant of Judge Richard Peters and a member of a wealthy family. Dana spent much of his adult life abroad, studying art and sight-seeing. Before the Civil War, he took classes at the royal academies in Dresden and Munich; and after the war, he traveled throughout Europe and the Middle East for almost twenty years. This extensive period abroad provided him with subjects for many of the watercolors that he exhibited at the Pennsylvania Academy of the Fine Arts after his return to Philadelphia in 1894. Dana served as president of both the Philadelphia Watercolor Club and the Fellowship of the Pennsylvania Academy.

Dana must have met Thomas Eakins through their connections with the Pennsylvania Academy. Dana studied briefly at the Academy in 1876, the year that Eakins began teaching at the school. Eakins, too, was an avid watercolorist. He exhibited both oil paintings and watercolors at the Academy's annual exhibitions. Best known for penetratingly realistic portraits, Eakins rarely flattered his sitters. Dana, who was not particularly pleased with the manner in which he was portrayed by Eakins, commented when he gave the painting to the Pennsylvania Academy: "I trust you will do justice to my absolute lack of personal vanity in permitting myself to go down to posterity in so unpleasant a presentment." With subtle emphasis on just a few details—the elegant cigarette holder, the coat of arms painted into the plain background, and, most of all the expression of the sitter—Eakins manages to convey a convincing image of cosmopolitan hauteur.

References:

Ernest Spofford, ed., *Encyclopedia of Pennsylvania Biography*, New York: Lewis Historical Publishing Co., 1928, vol. 14, pp. 223-224.

Lloyd Goodrich, *Thomas Eakins, His Life and Work*, New York: Whitney Museum of American Art, 1933, no. 367.

The entries in this catalogue provide a short list of references for each artist. The following books are useful for more general reading related to nineteenth-century American portraiture.

American Folk Portraits, Paintings and Drawings from the Abby Aldrich Rockefeller Folk Art Center. Boston: New York Graphic Society, 1981.

American Portraits. Exhib. cat. Philadelphia: Frank S. Schwarz and Son, 1985.

Artists By Themselves, Artists' Portraits from the National Academy of Design. Exhib. cat. New York: National Academy of Design, 1983.

Calvert, Karin. "Children in American Family Portraiture, 1670 to 1810." *William and Mary Quarterly* 39 (Jan. 1982), pp. 87-113.

A Catalogue of American Portraits in the New-York Historical Society. 2 vols. New Haven, Conn.: Yale University Press, 1974.

Christman, Margaret C. *Fifty American Faces from the Collection of the National Portrait Gallery.* Washington, D. C.: Smithsonian Institution Press, 1978.

The Classical Spirit in American Portraiture. Exhib. cat. Providence, R. I.: Bell Gallery, Brown University, 1976.

Craven, Wayne. *Colonial American Portraiture.* Cambridge: Cambridge University Press, 1986.

Deutsch, Davida Tenenbaum. "The Polite Lady: Portraits of American School Girls and their Accomplishments." *Antiques* 135 (March 1989), pp. 742-753.

Fabian, Monroe. *Portraits of the American State, 1771-1971.* Exhib. cat. National Portrait Gallery, Washington, D. C.: Smithsonian Institution Press, 1971.

Hennessey, John. *The American Portrait: From the Death of Stuart to the Rise of Sargent.* Exhib. cat. Worcester, Mass.: Worcester Art Museum, 1973.

Heslip, Colleen Cowles. *Between the Rivers, Itinerant Painters from the Connecticut to the Hudson.* Exhib. cat. Williamstown, Mass.: Sterling and Francine Clark Art Institute, 1990.

Lipton, Leah. "William Dunlap, Samuel F. B. Morse, John Wesley Jarvis, and Chester Harding: Their Careers as Itinerant Portrait Painters." *American Art Journal* 13 (Summer 1981), pp. 34-50.

Lubin, David. *Act of Portrayal, Eakins, Sargent, and James.* New Haven, Conn.: Yale University Press, 1985.

McCandless, Barbara. "The Portrait Studio and the Celebrity." In *Photography in Nineteenth-Century America.* Exhib. cat. Fort Worth: Amon Carter Museum, 1991, pp. 49-75.

Miles, Ellen. "Great American Profile: folk portraiture reconsidered." *Art Journal* 39 (Summer 1980), pp. 279-281.

Philadelphia Portraiture: 1740-1910. Exhib. cat. Philadelphia: Frank S. Schwarz and Sons, 1982.

Praz, Mario. *Conversation Pieces, A Survey of the Informal Group Portrait in Europe and America.* University Park, Pa.: Pennsylvania State University Press, 1971.

Quick, Michael, et al. *American Portraiture in the Grand Manner: 1720-1920.* Exhib. cat. Los Angeles: Los Angeles County Museum of Art, 1981.

Saunders, Richard H., and Ellen G. Miles. *American Colonial Portraits, 1700-1776.* Washington, D. C.: Smithsonian Institution Press, 1987.

Schorsch, Anita. *Images of Childhood, An Illustrated Social History.* Pittstown, N. J.: Main Street Press, 1985.

Sears, Clara Endicott. *Some American Primitives, A Study of New England Faces and Folk Portraits.* Boston: Houghton Mifflin Co., 1941.

Simon, Robin. *The Portrait in Britain and America.* Boston: G. K. Hall, 1987.

Stewart, Robert G. *A Nineteenth-Century Gallery of Distinguished Americans.* Exhib. cat. Washington, D. C.: Smithsonian Institution Press, 1969.

Strickler, Susan E. *American Portrait Miniatures.* Worcester, Mass.: Worcester Art Museum, 1989.

Townsend, J. Benjamin, ed. *This New Man: A Discourse in Portraits.* Exhib. cat. Washington, D. C.: Smithsonian Institution Press, 1968.

Van Devanter, Ann C., and Alfred V. Frankenstein. *American Self-Portraits.* Exhib. cat. New York: E. P. Dutton for International Exhibitions Foundation, 1974.

Vlach, John Michael. *Plain Painters, Making Sense of American Folk Art.* Washington, D. C.: Smithsonian Institution Press, 1988.